Karen's
Color It Your Way
Coloring Book

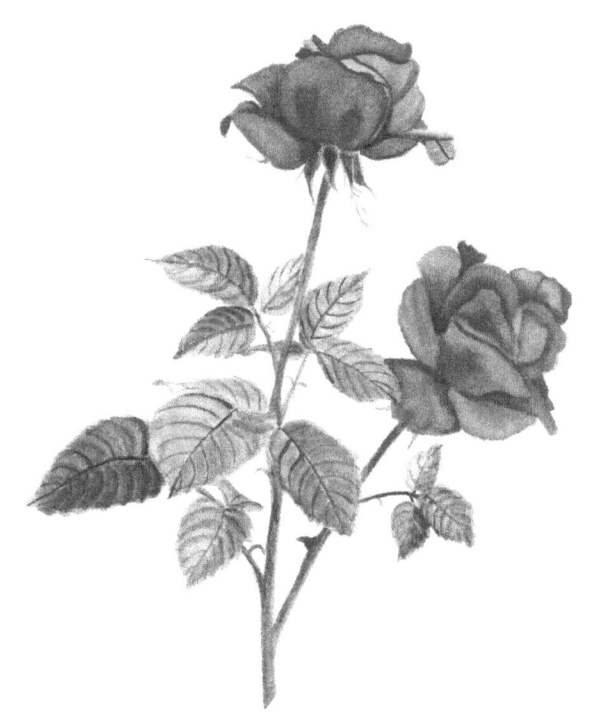

CHALLENGES YOU TO
FIND YOUR OWN LIGHT SOURCE, LIGHTS AND DARKS,
DISTANCE COLOR, FORM, AND COLOR CHOICE.
HAVE FUN.

Quality Graphics Production Assistance by Ronald Lee Hilde

Graphics to Publication Assistance by Jon Hilde

Copyright © 2018 Karen Hilde
All rights reserved.
ISBN: 1729732313
ISBN-13: 978-1729732311

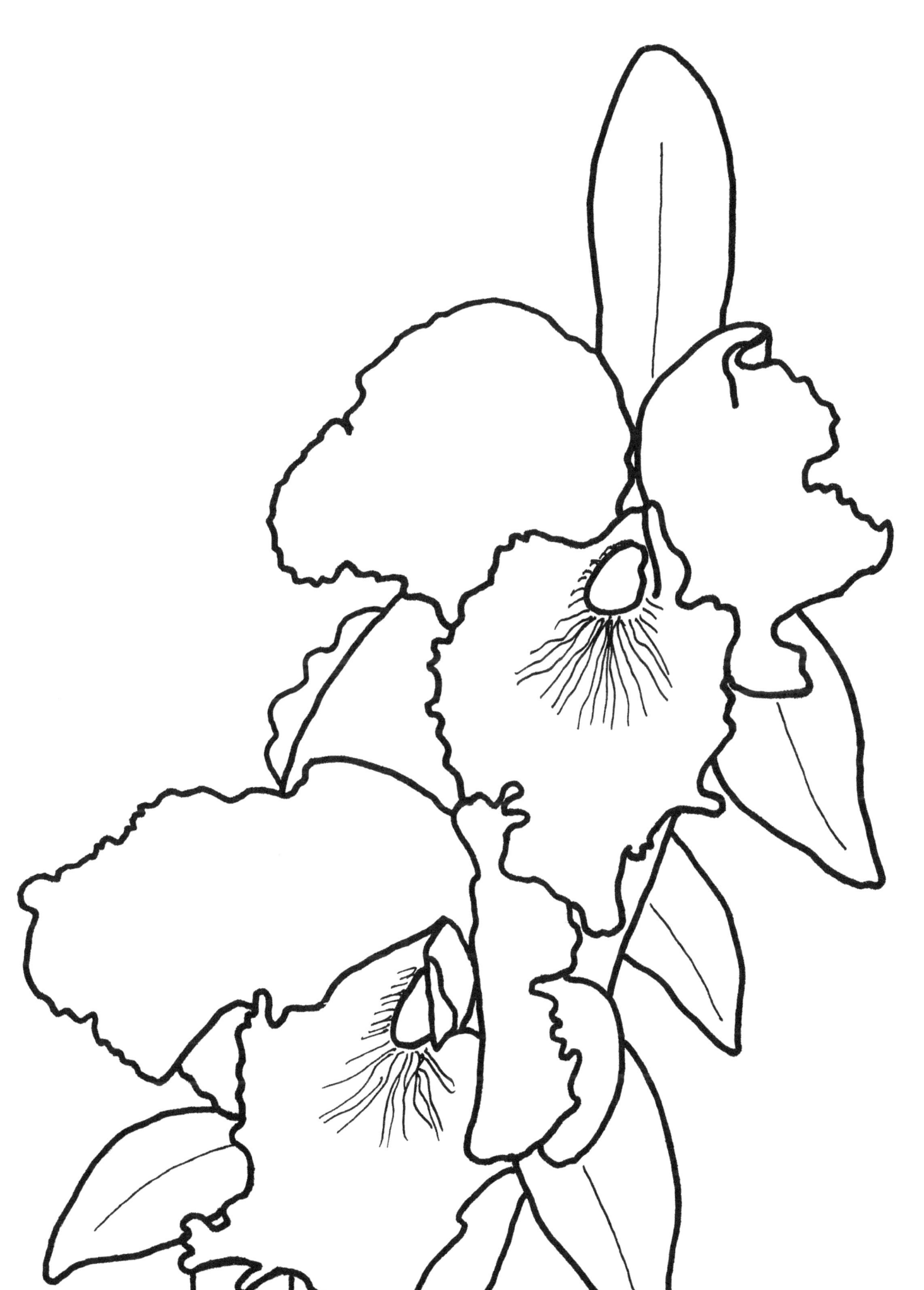

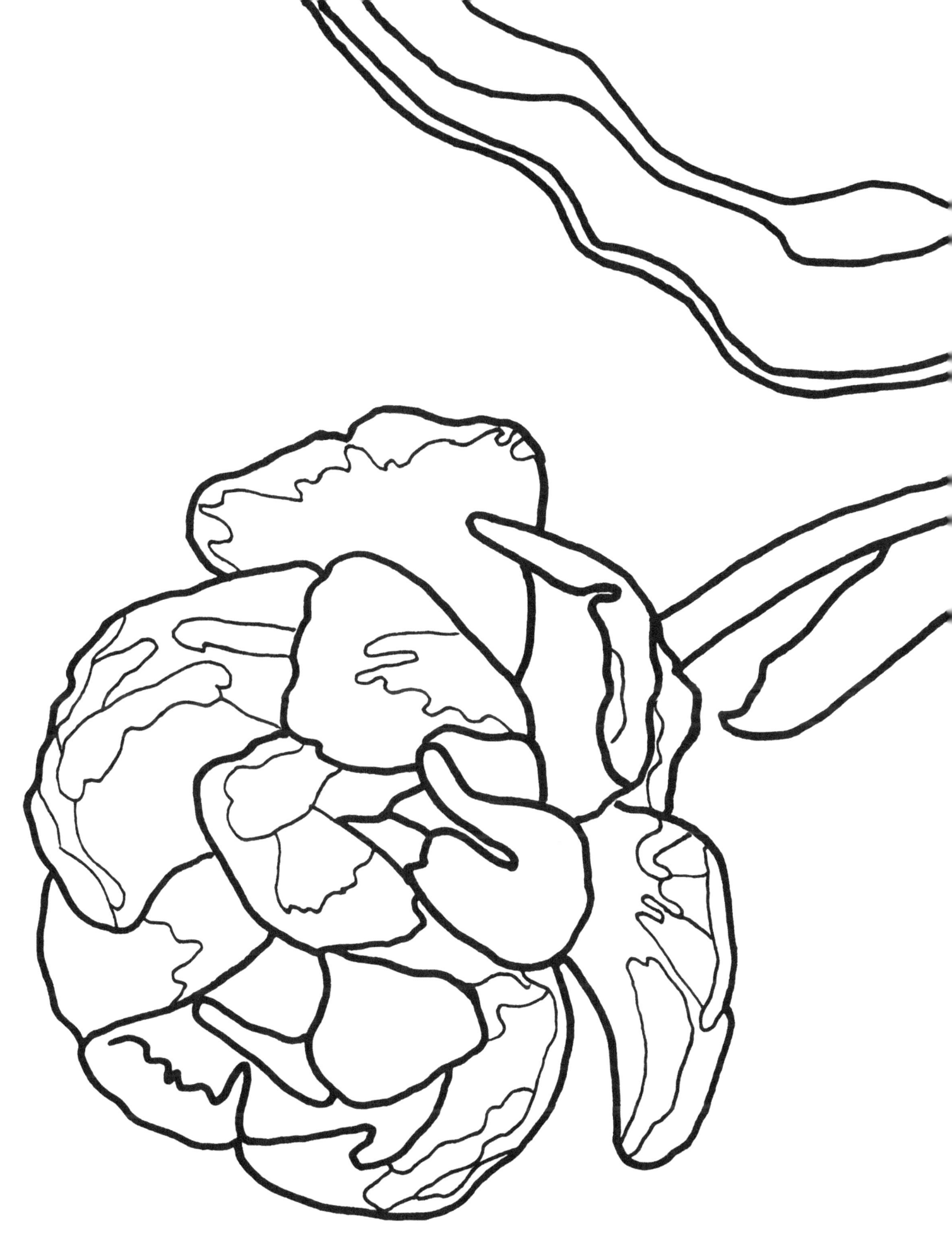

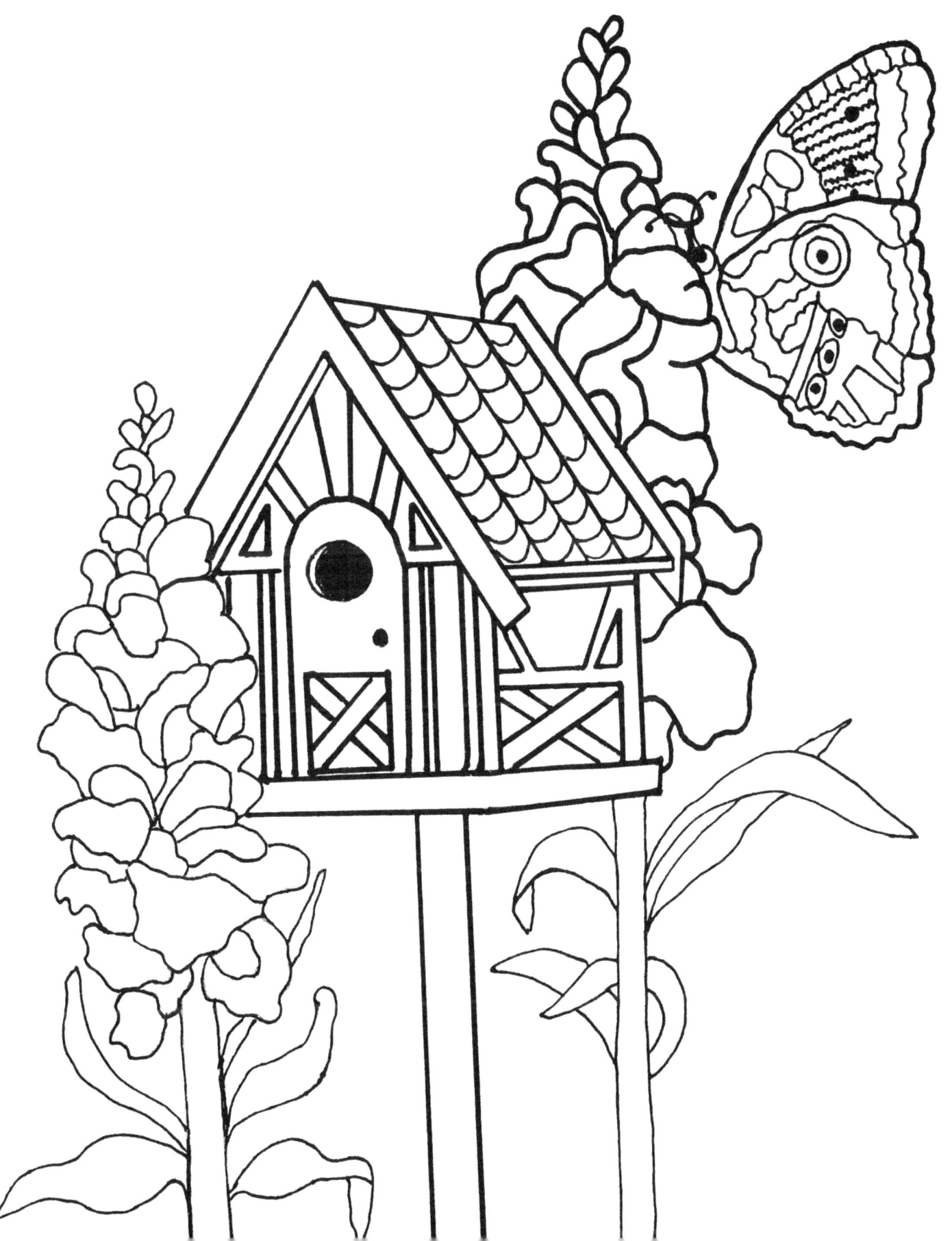

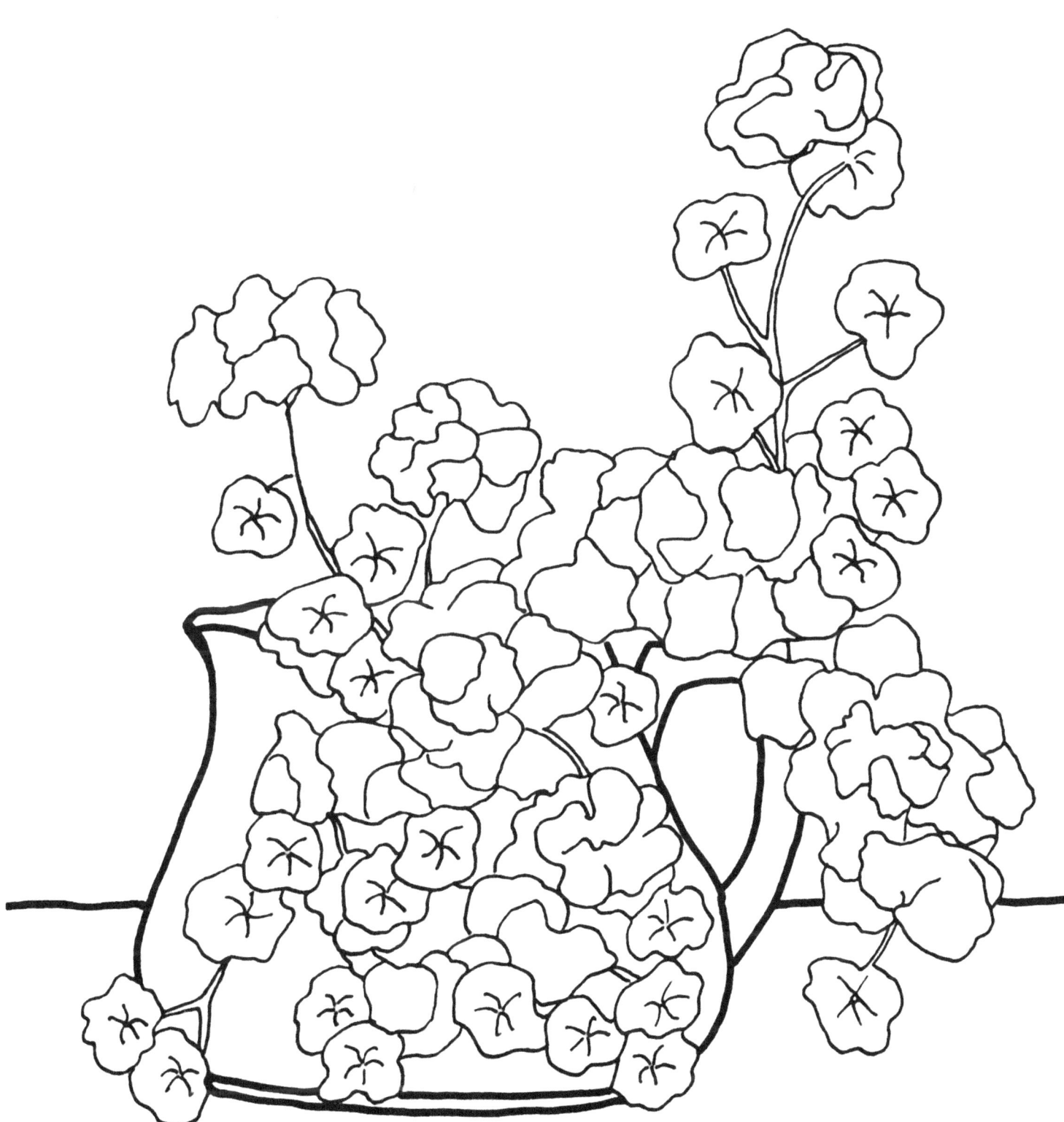

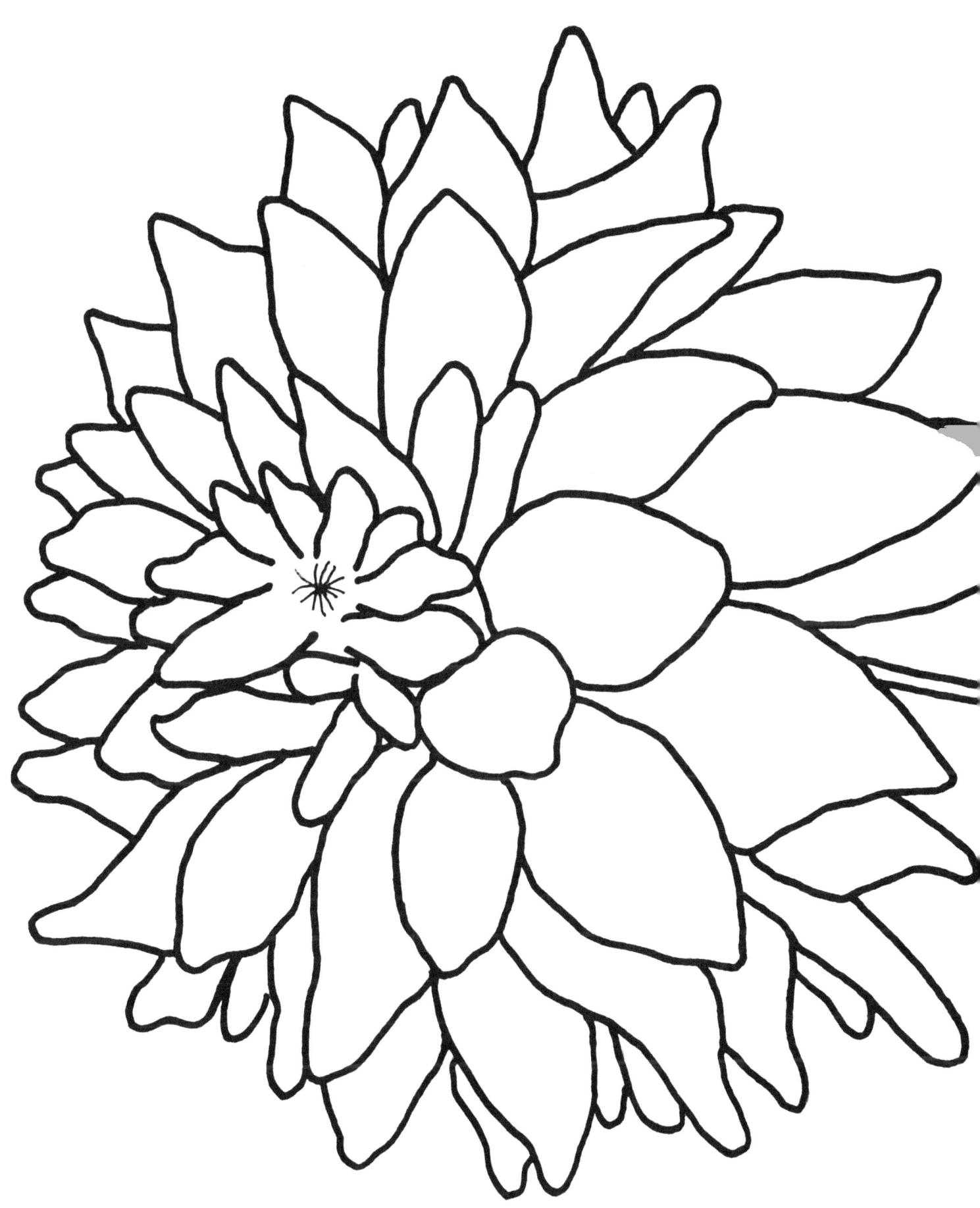

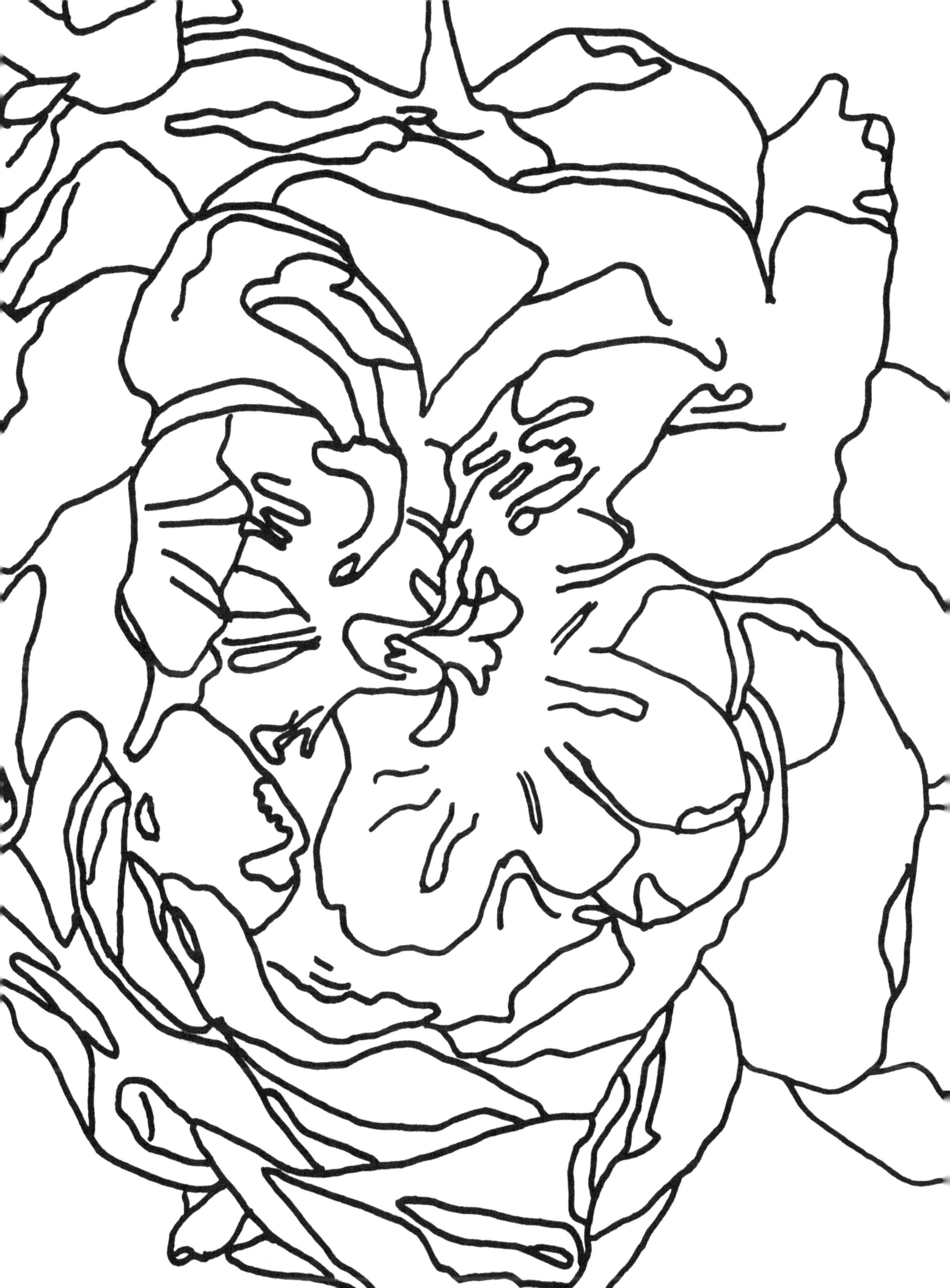

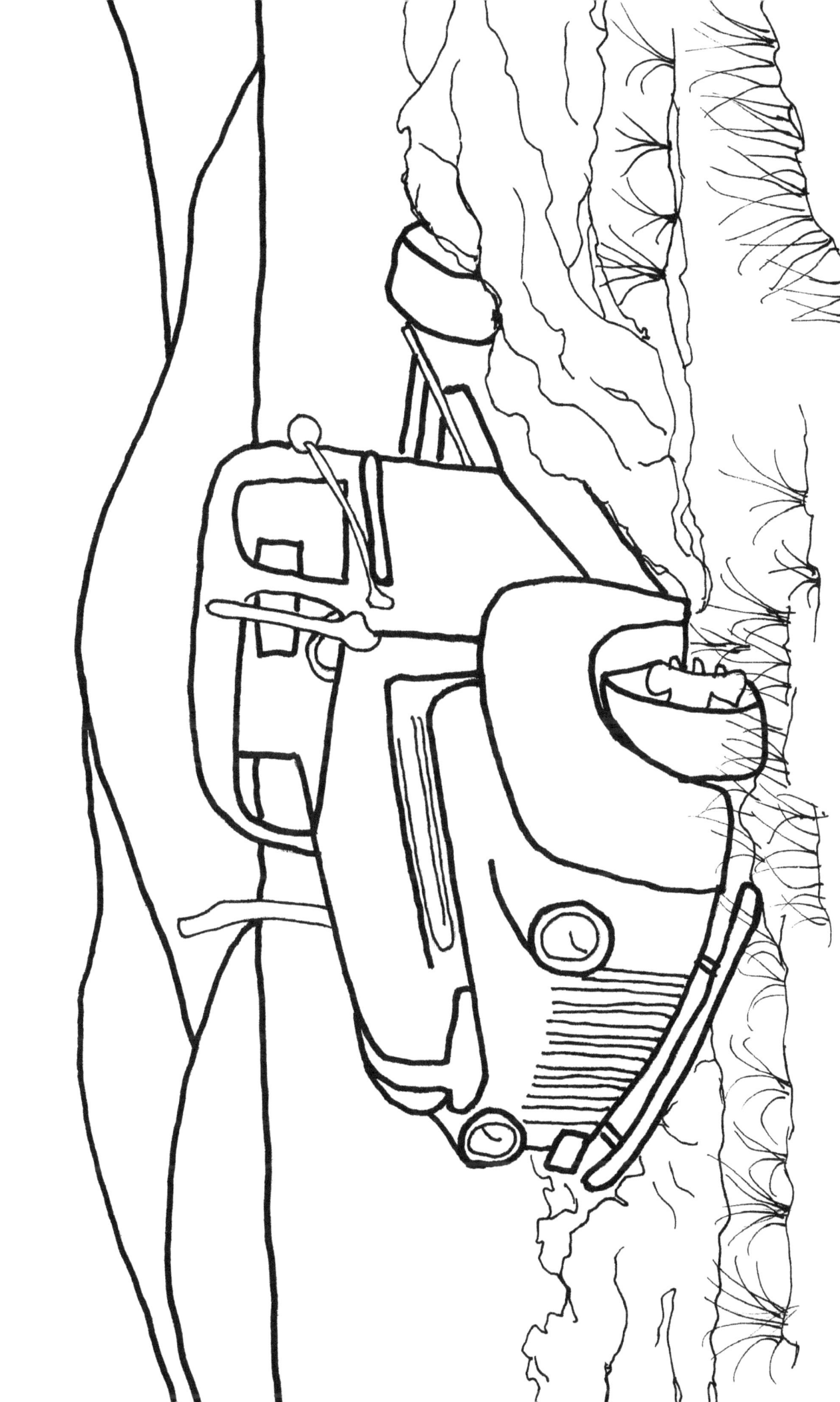

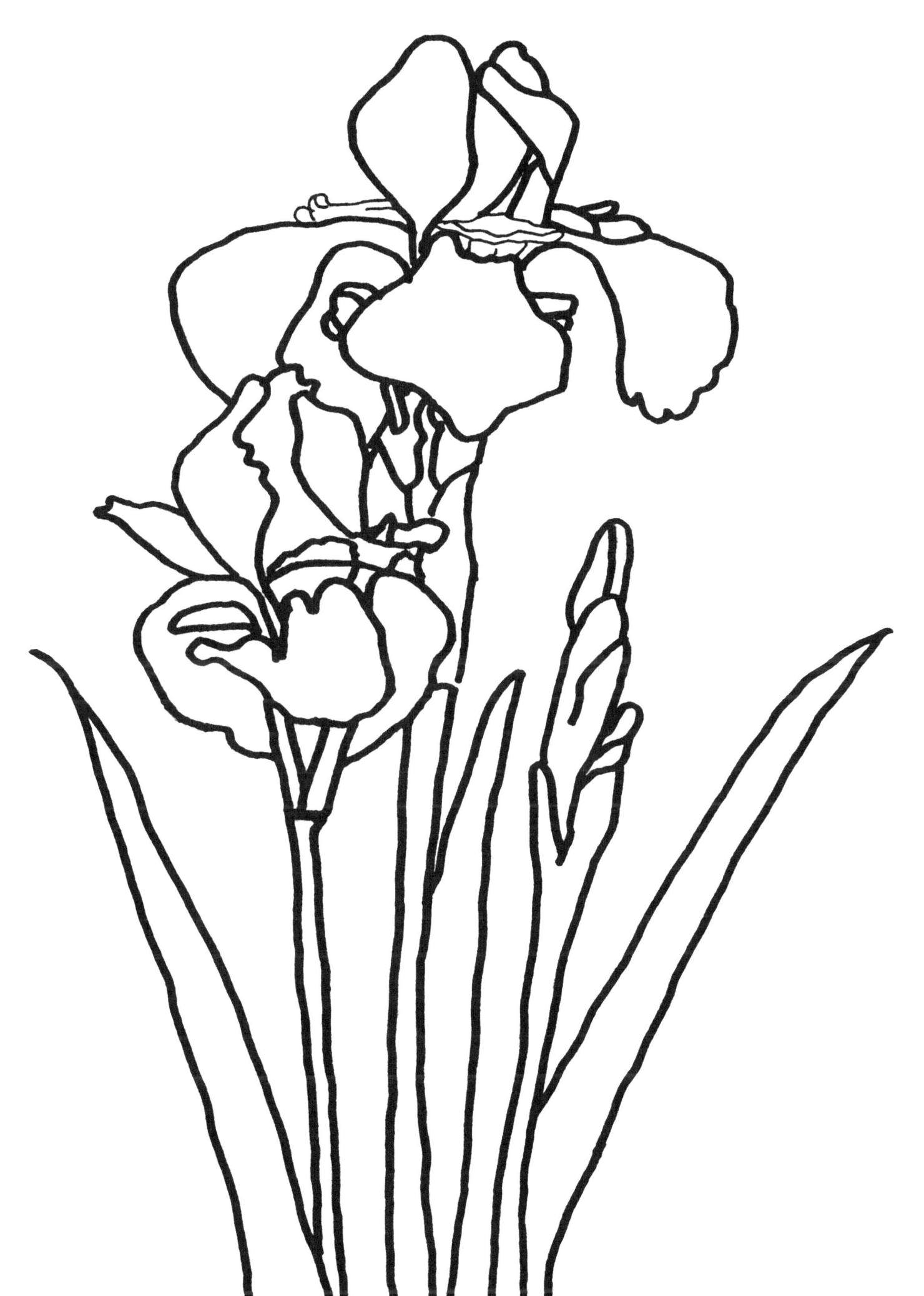

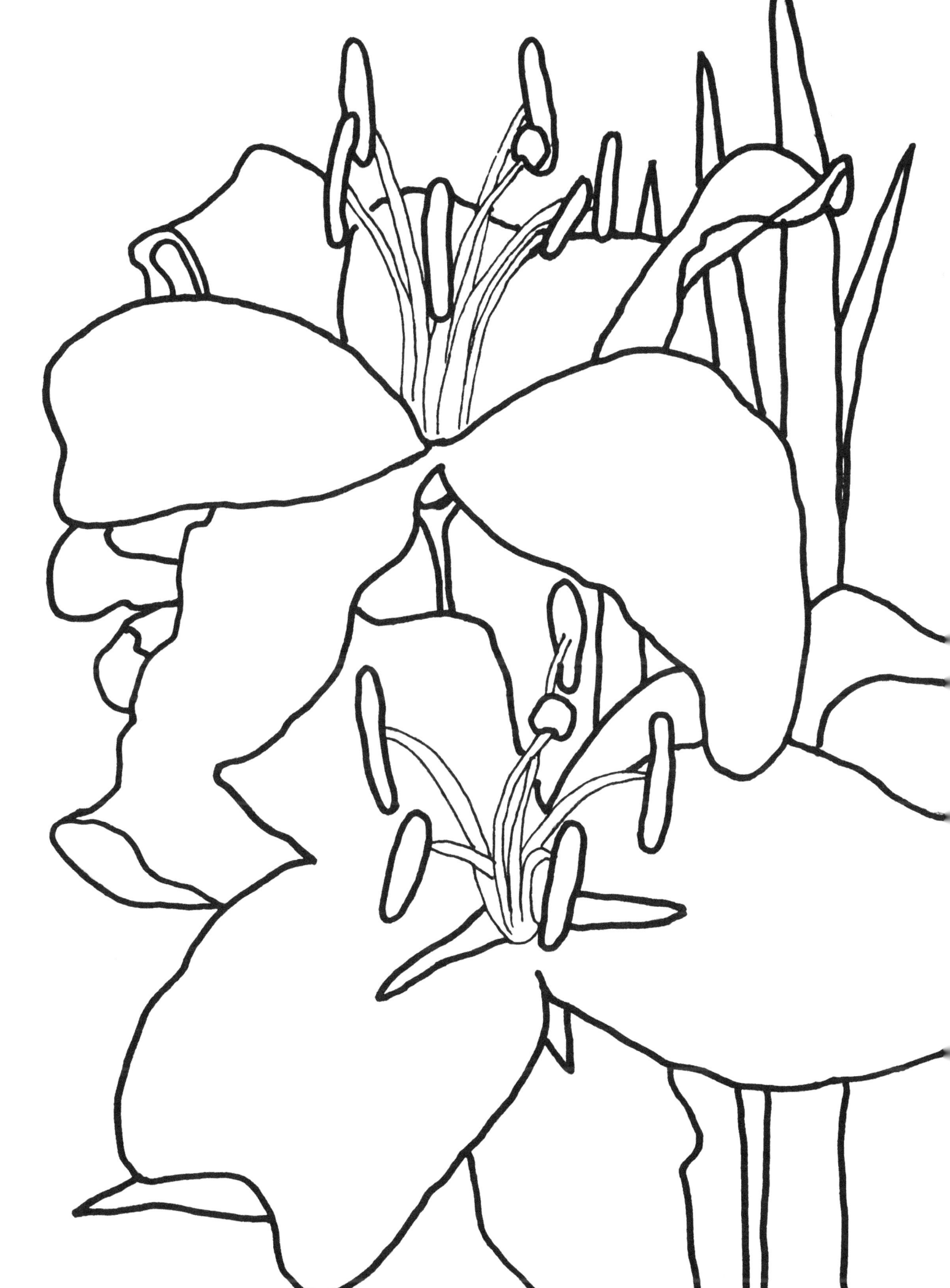

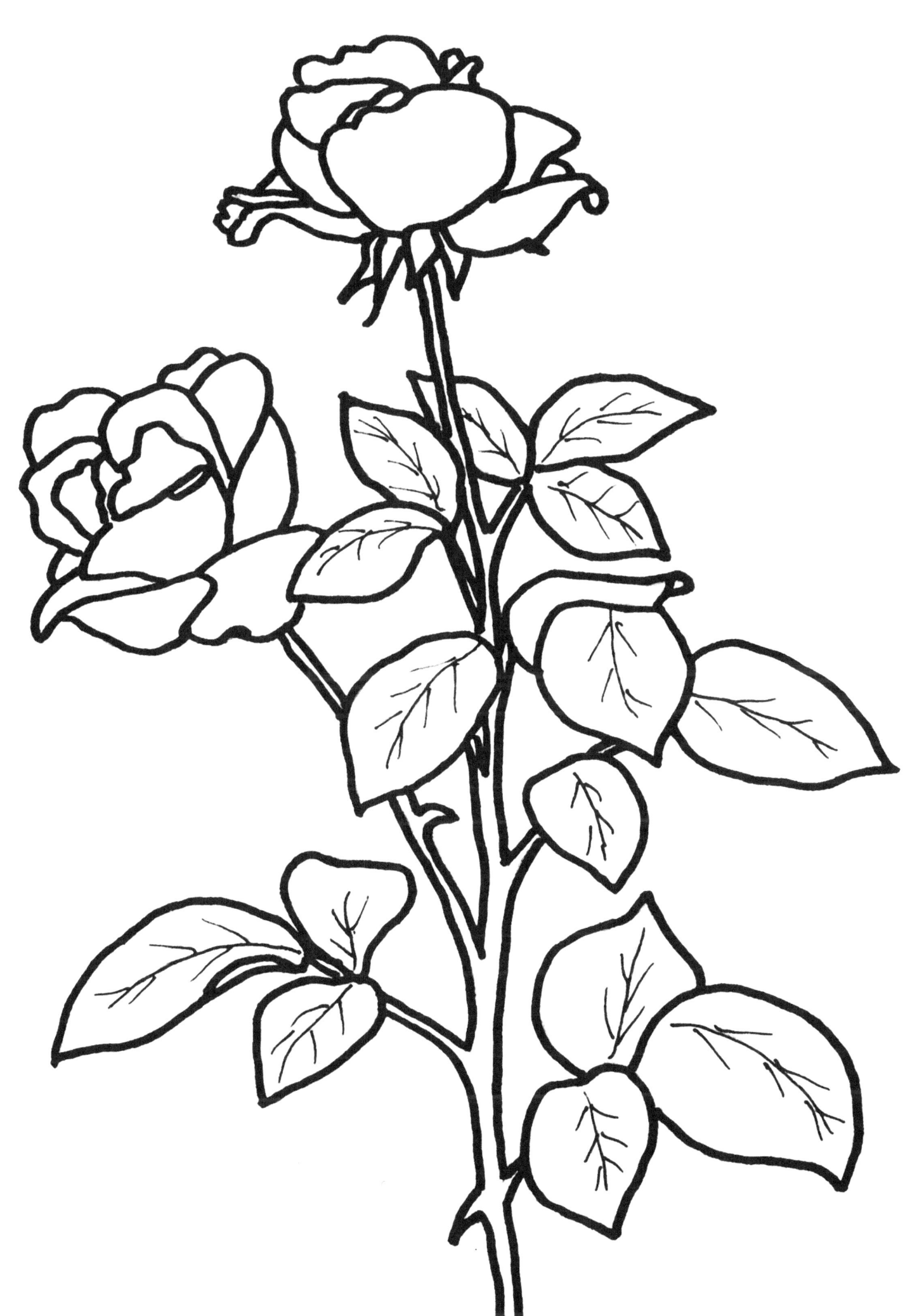

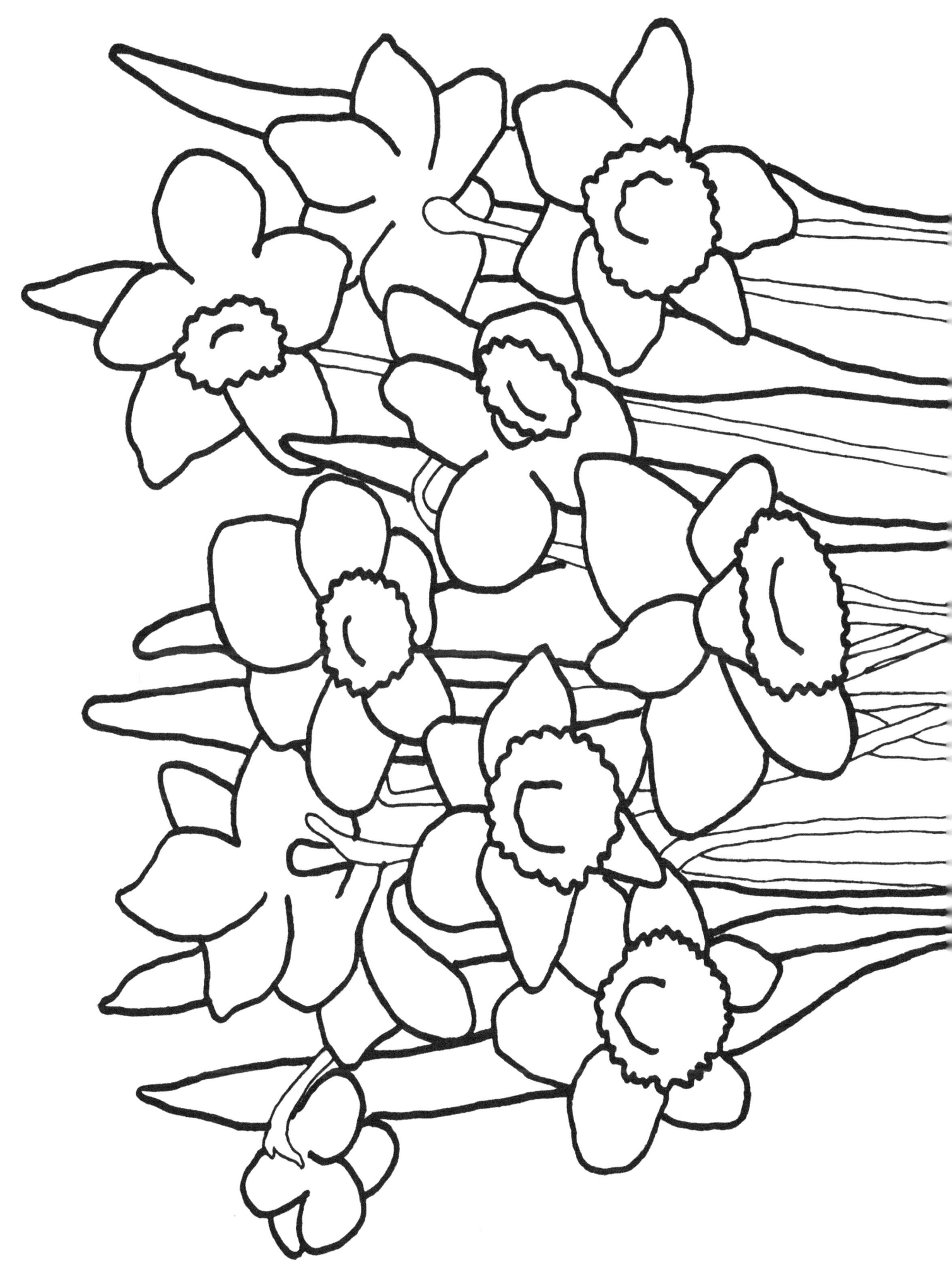

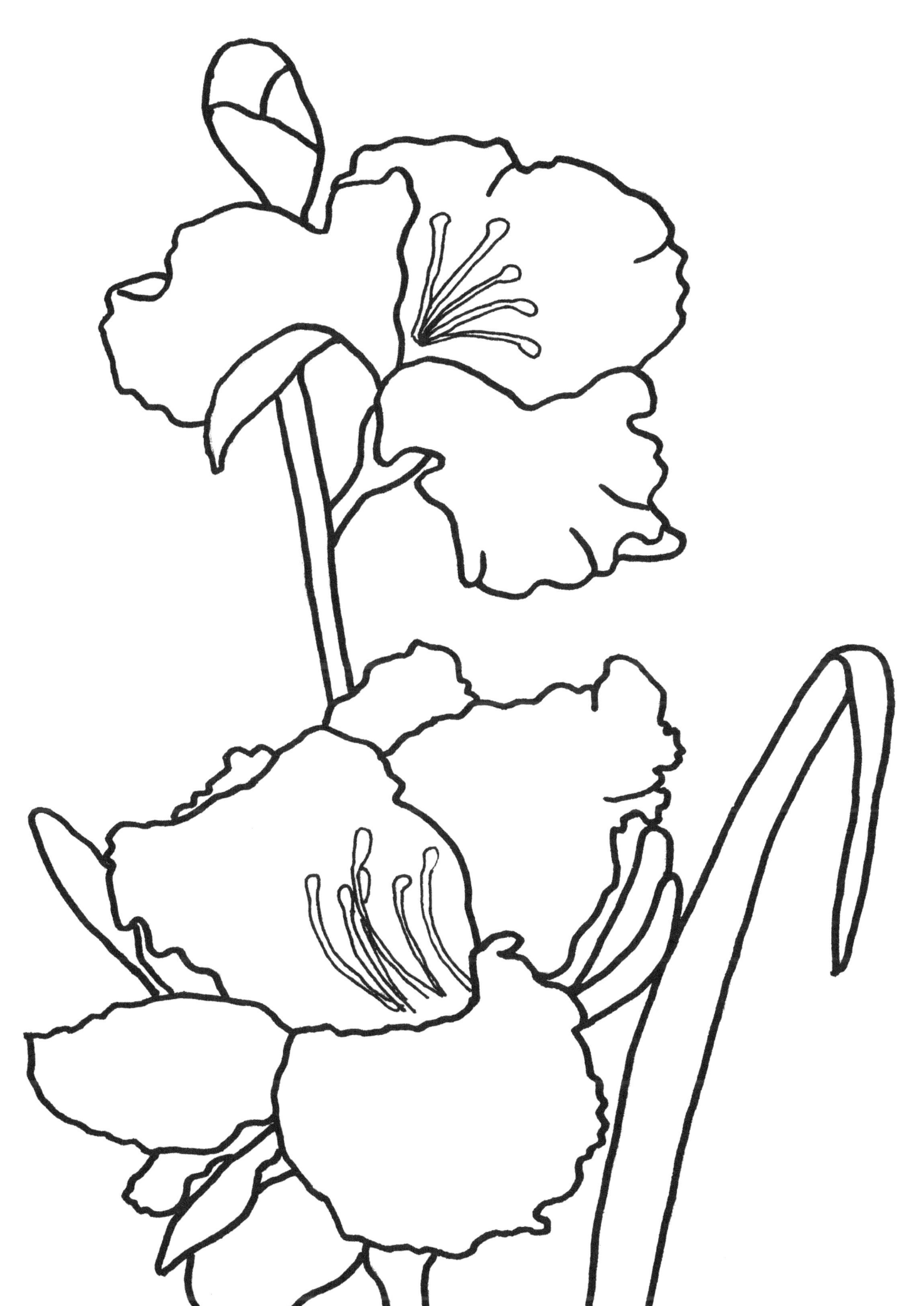

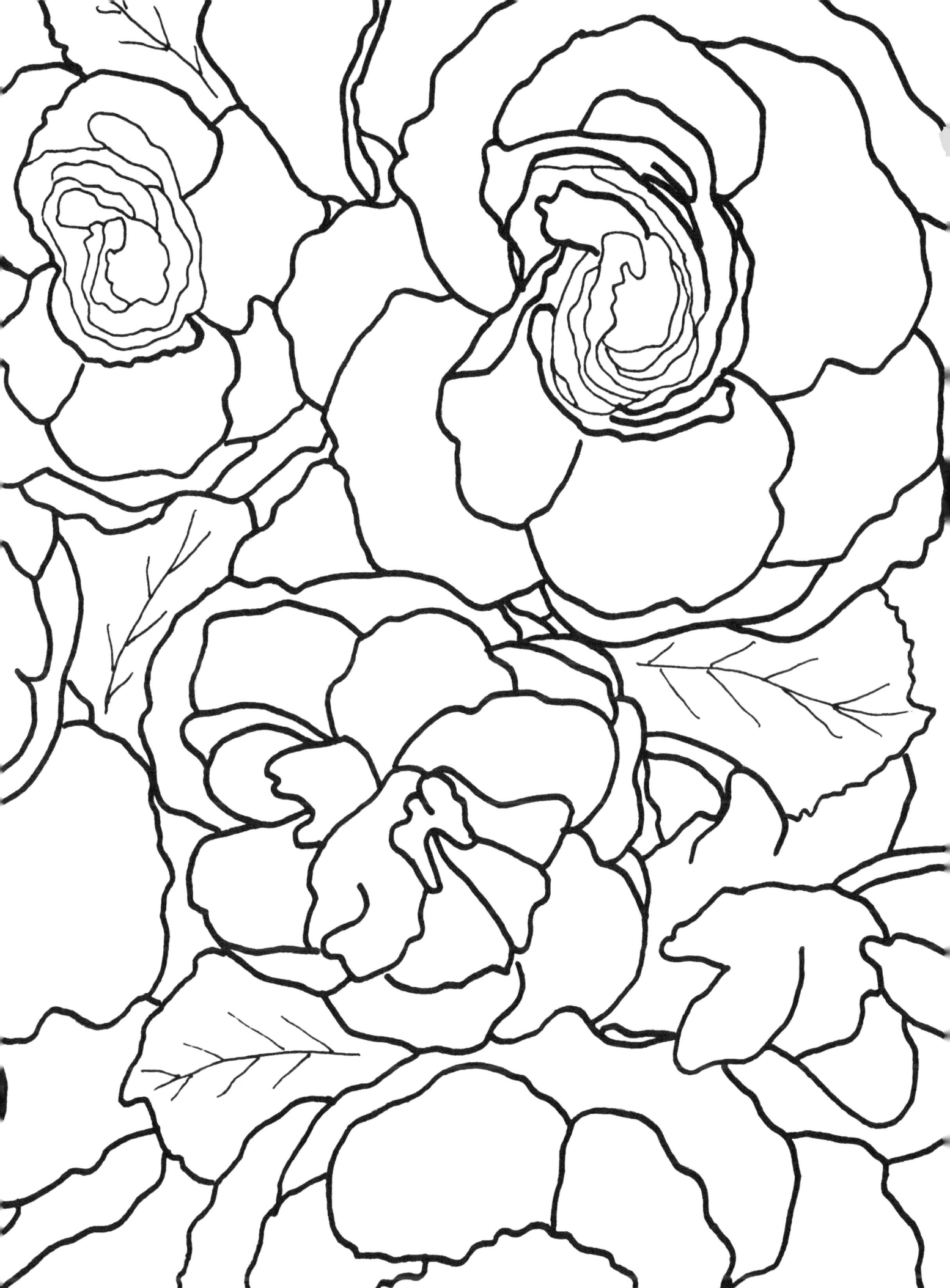

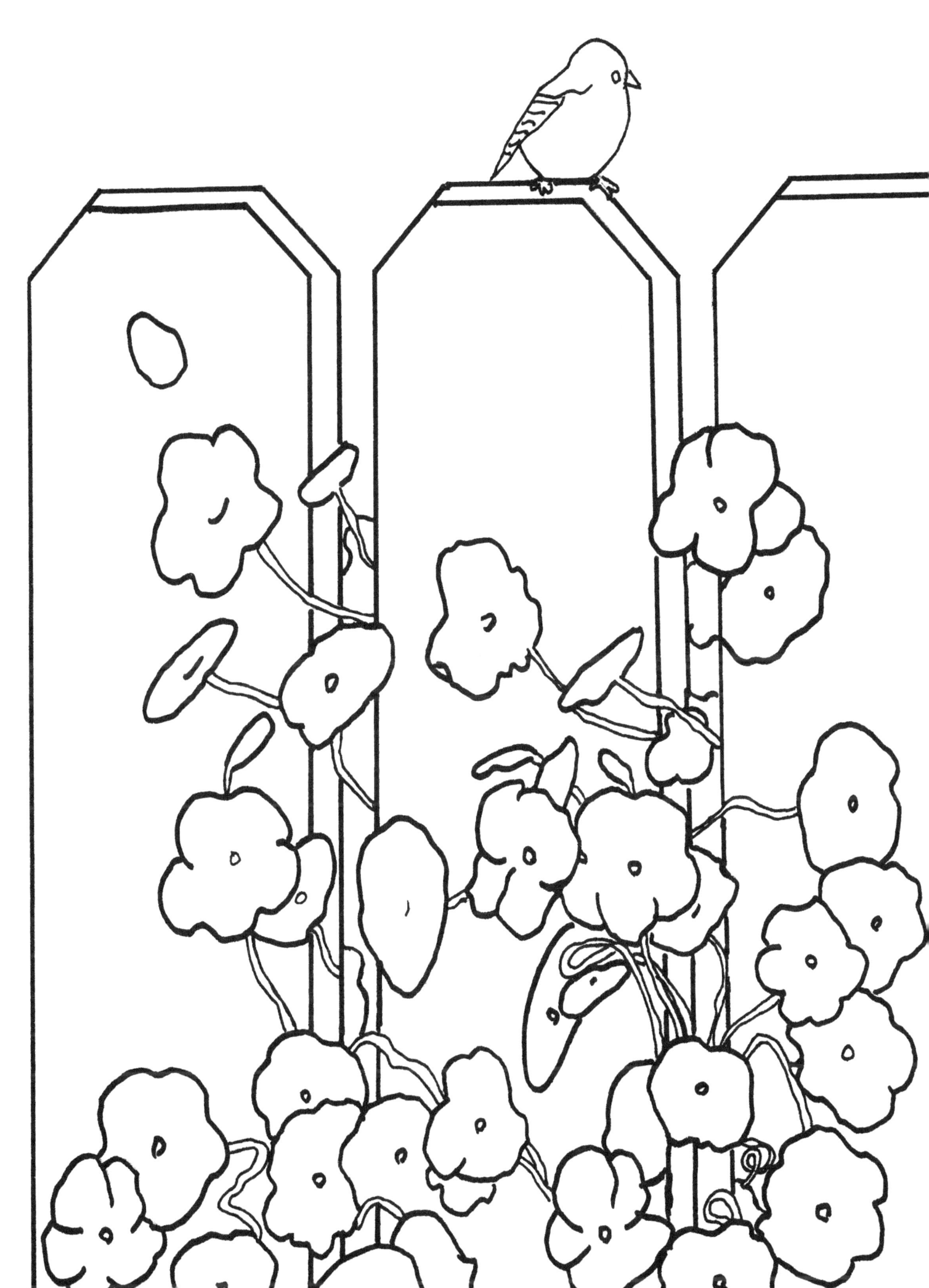

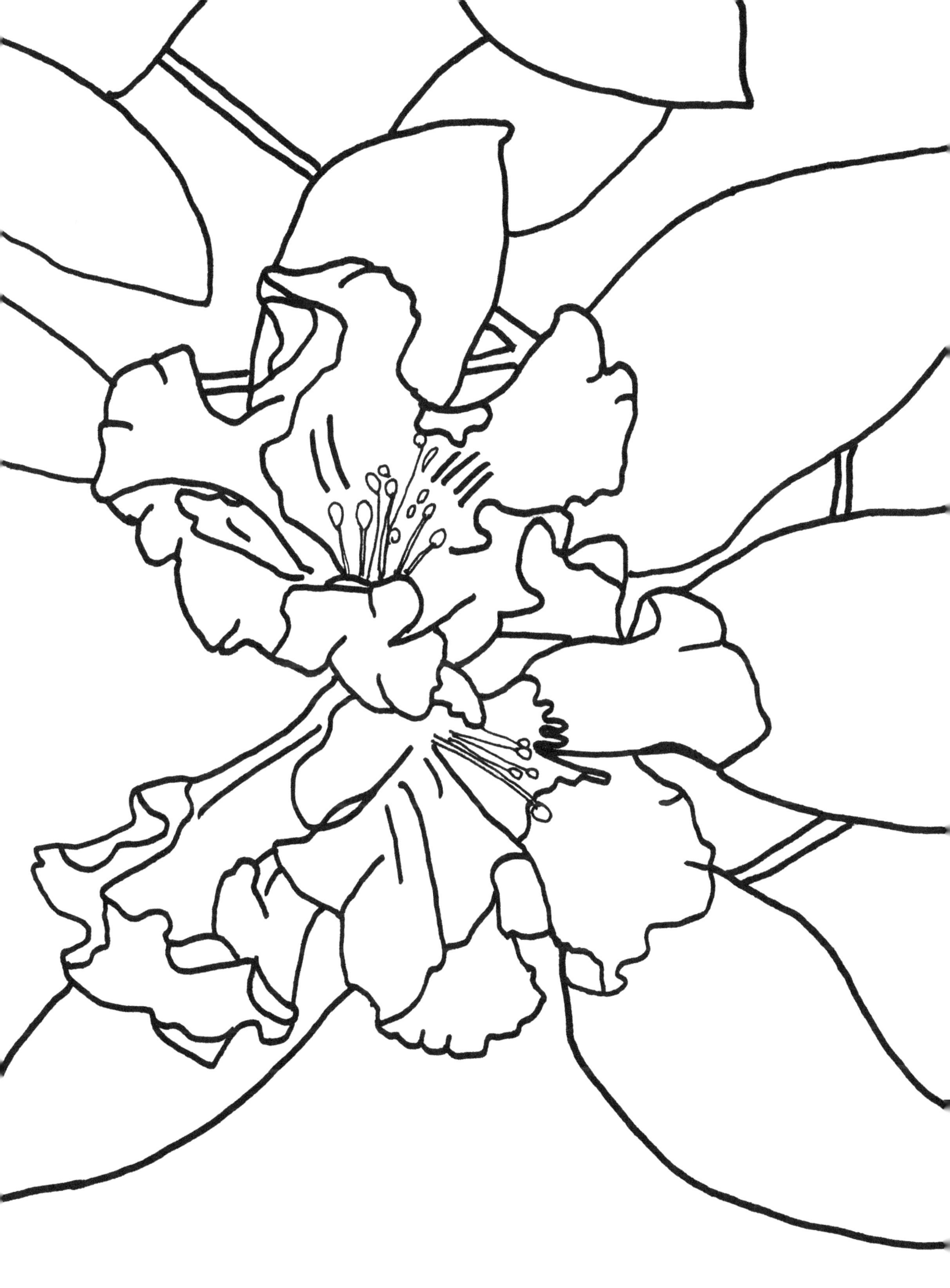

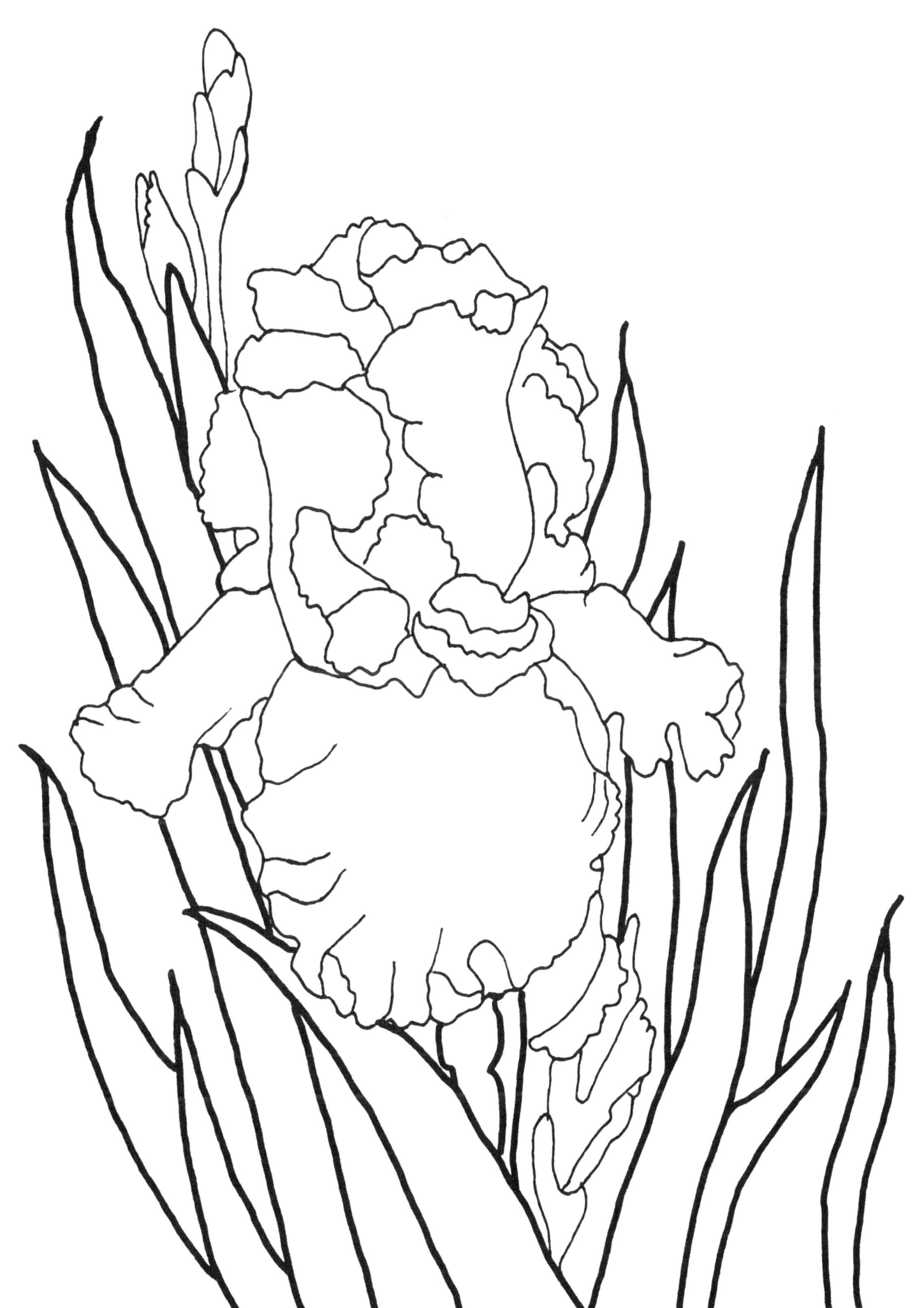

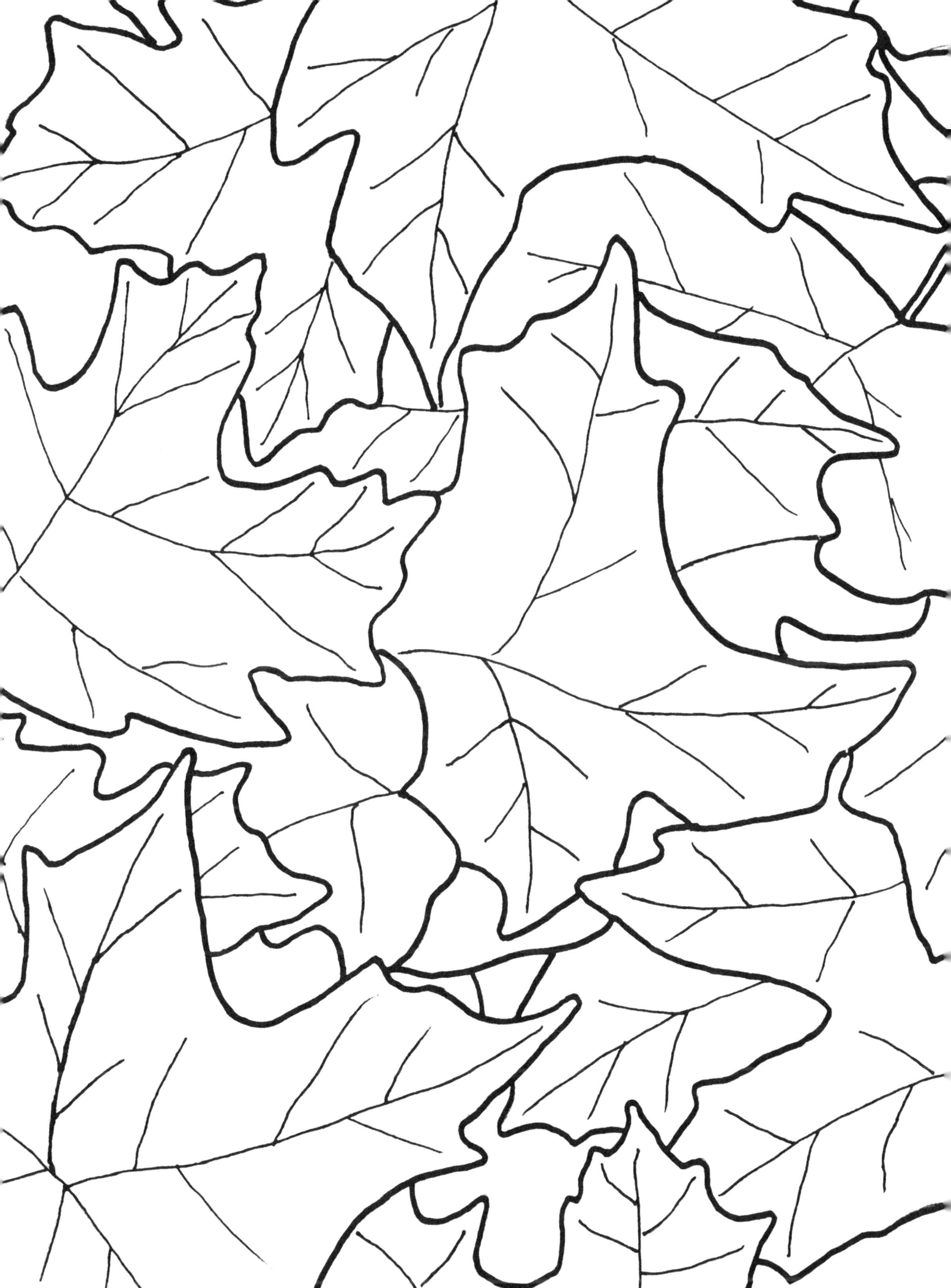

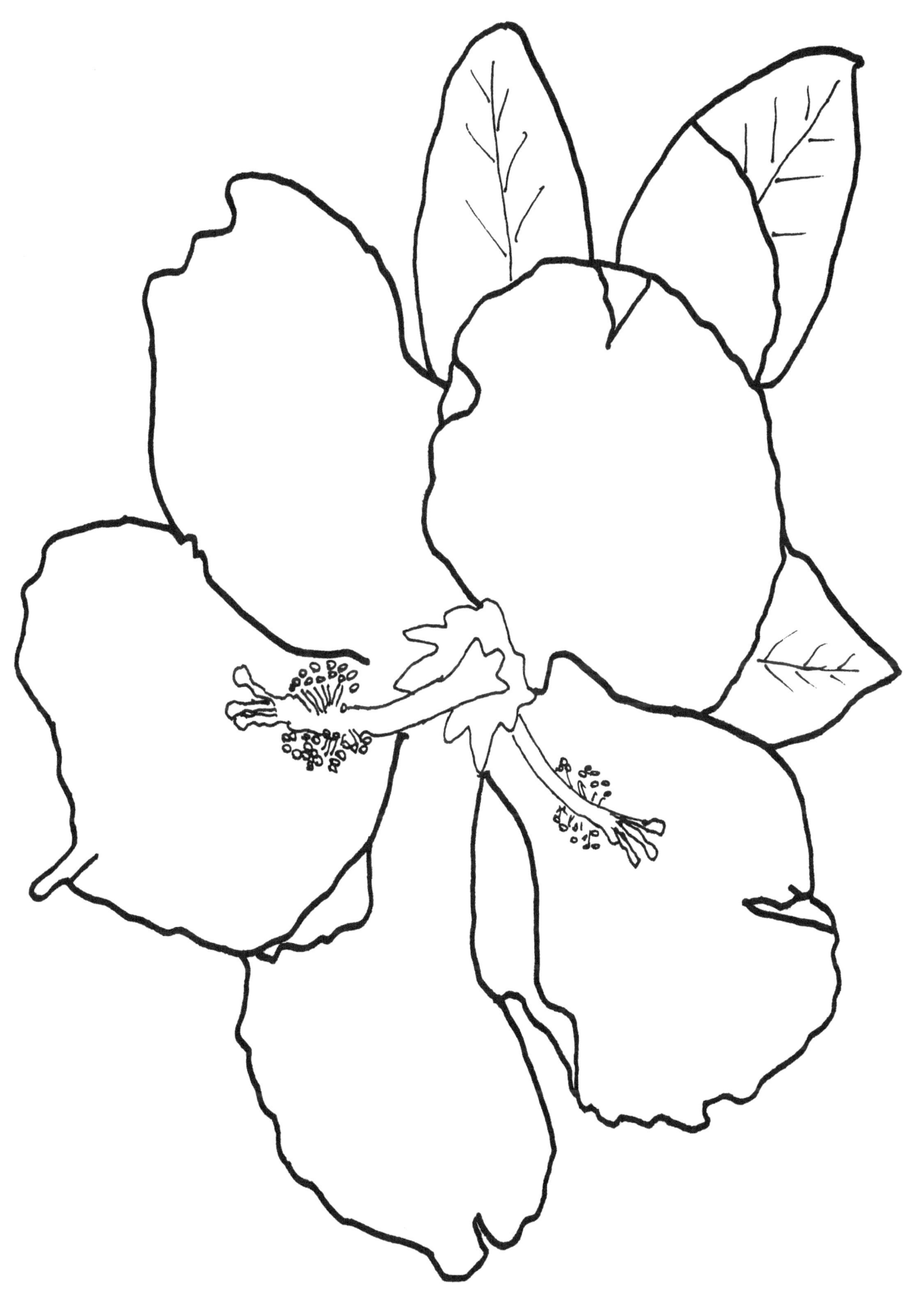

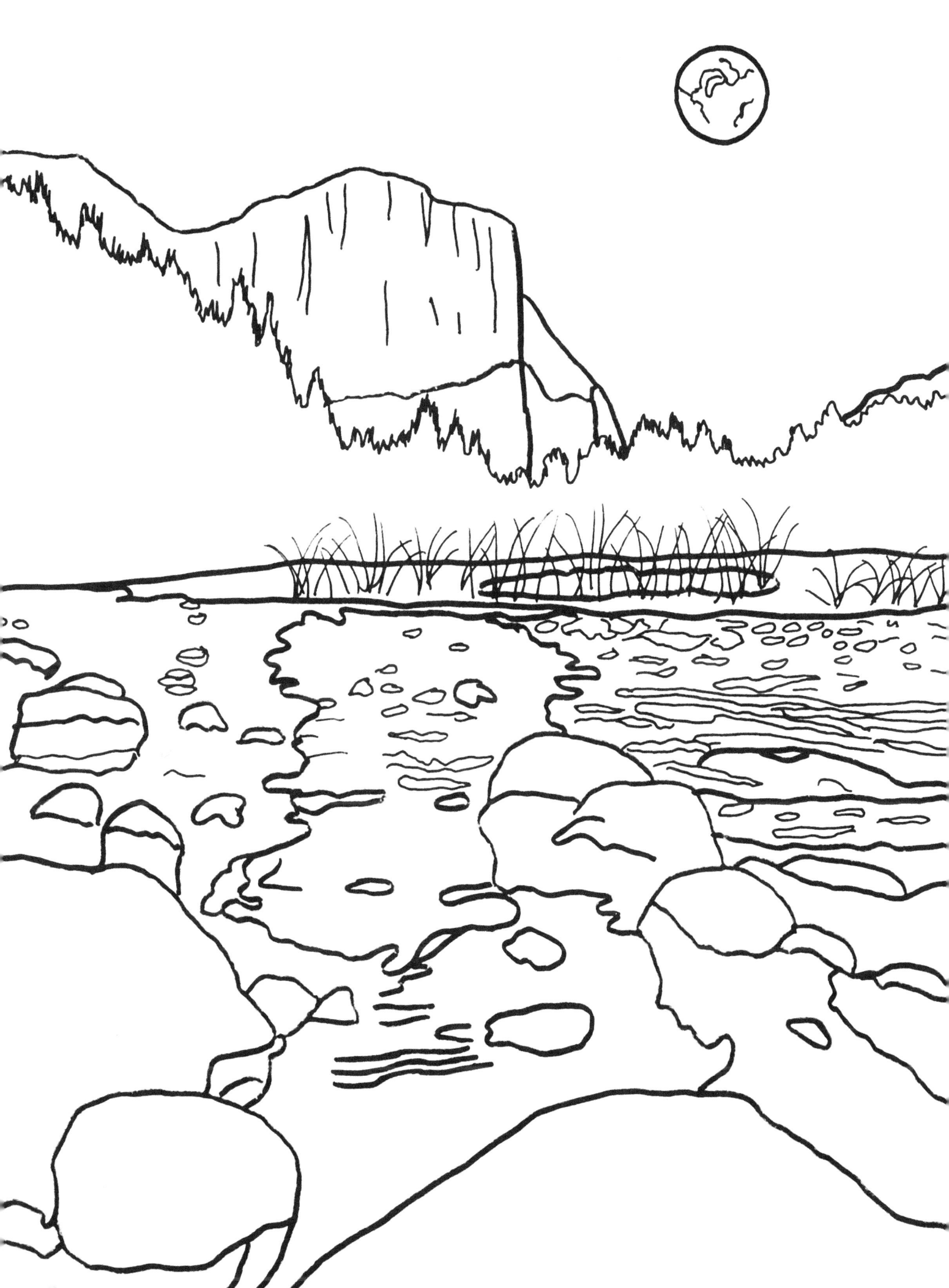

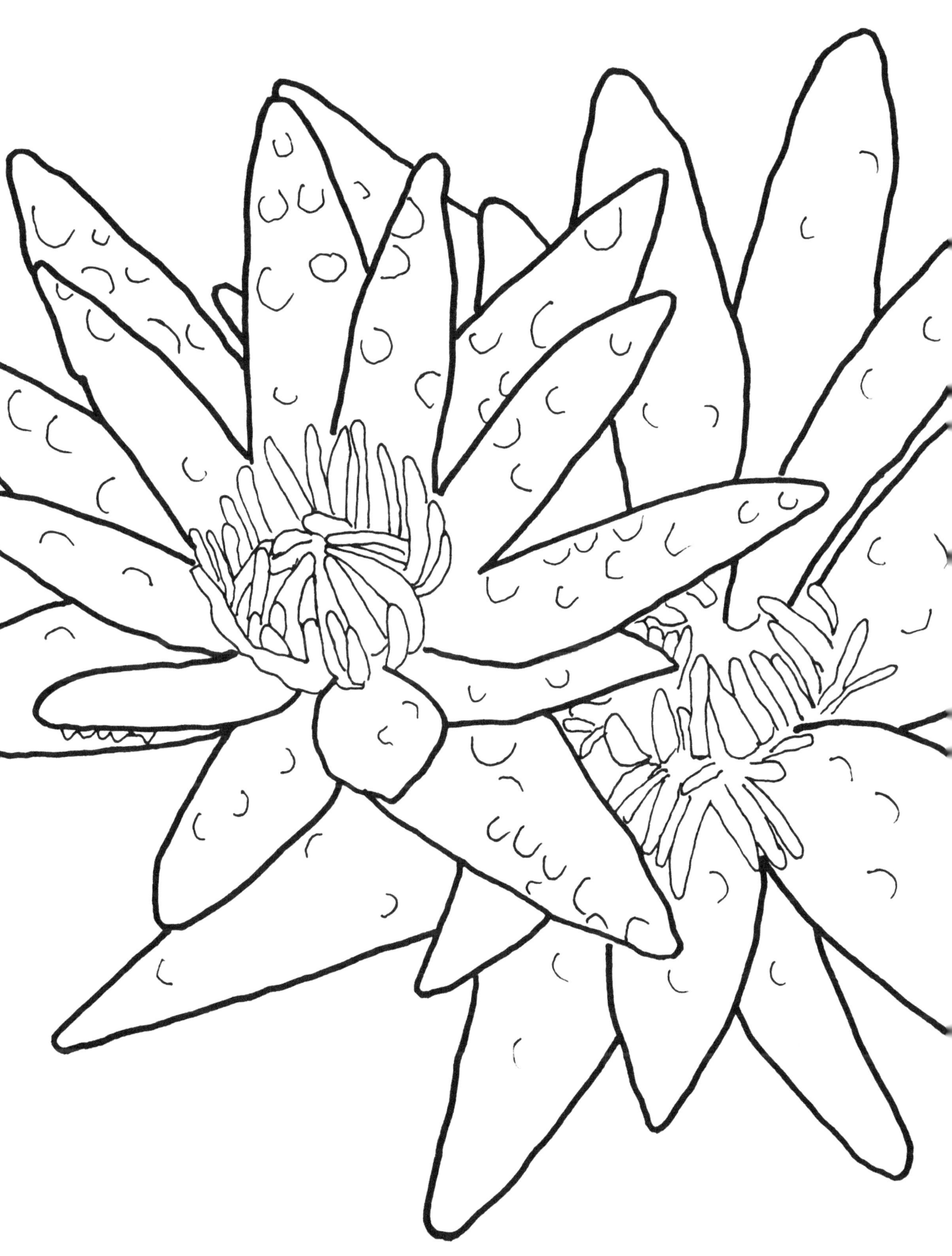

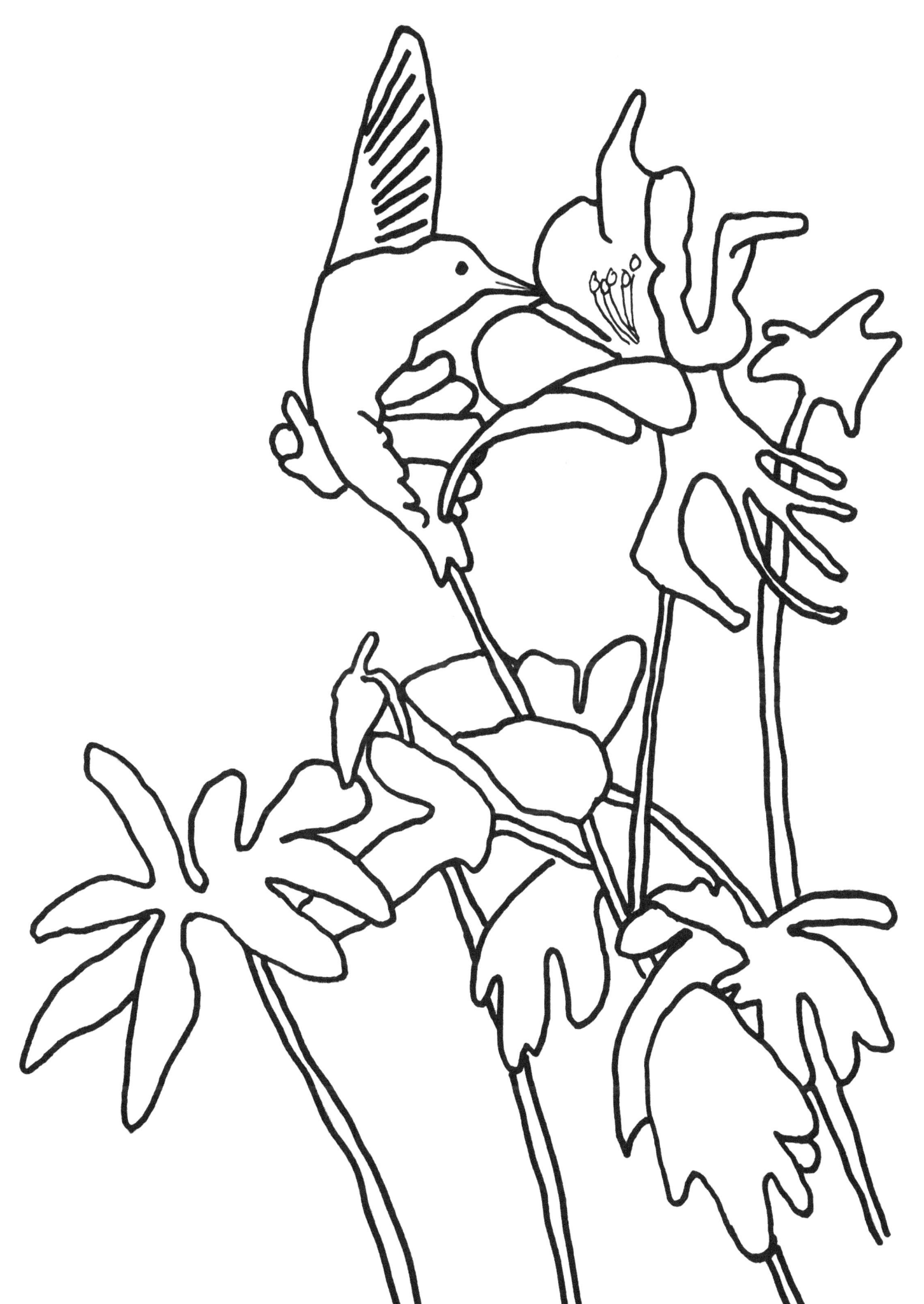

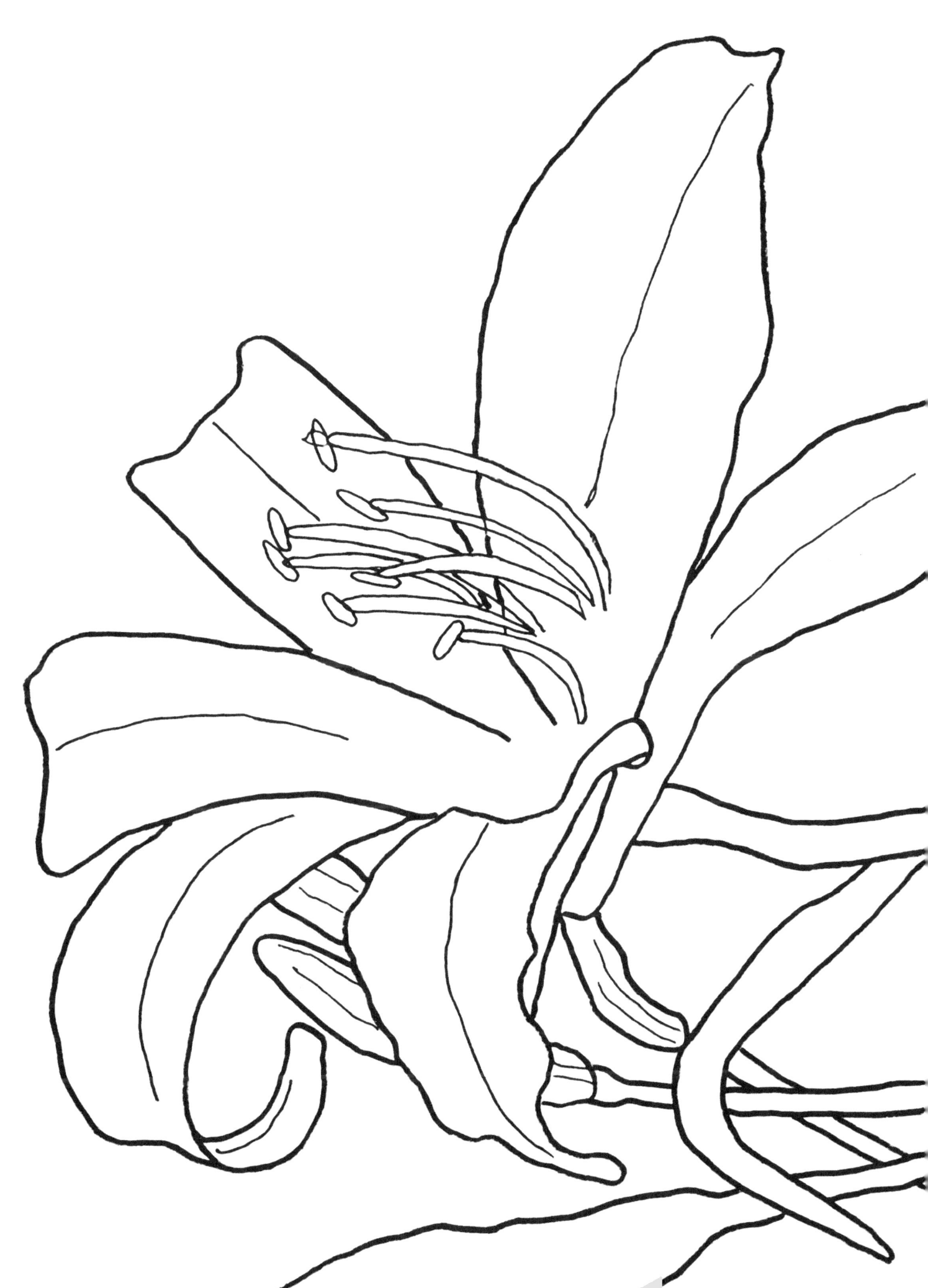

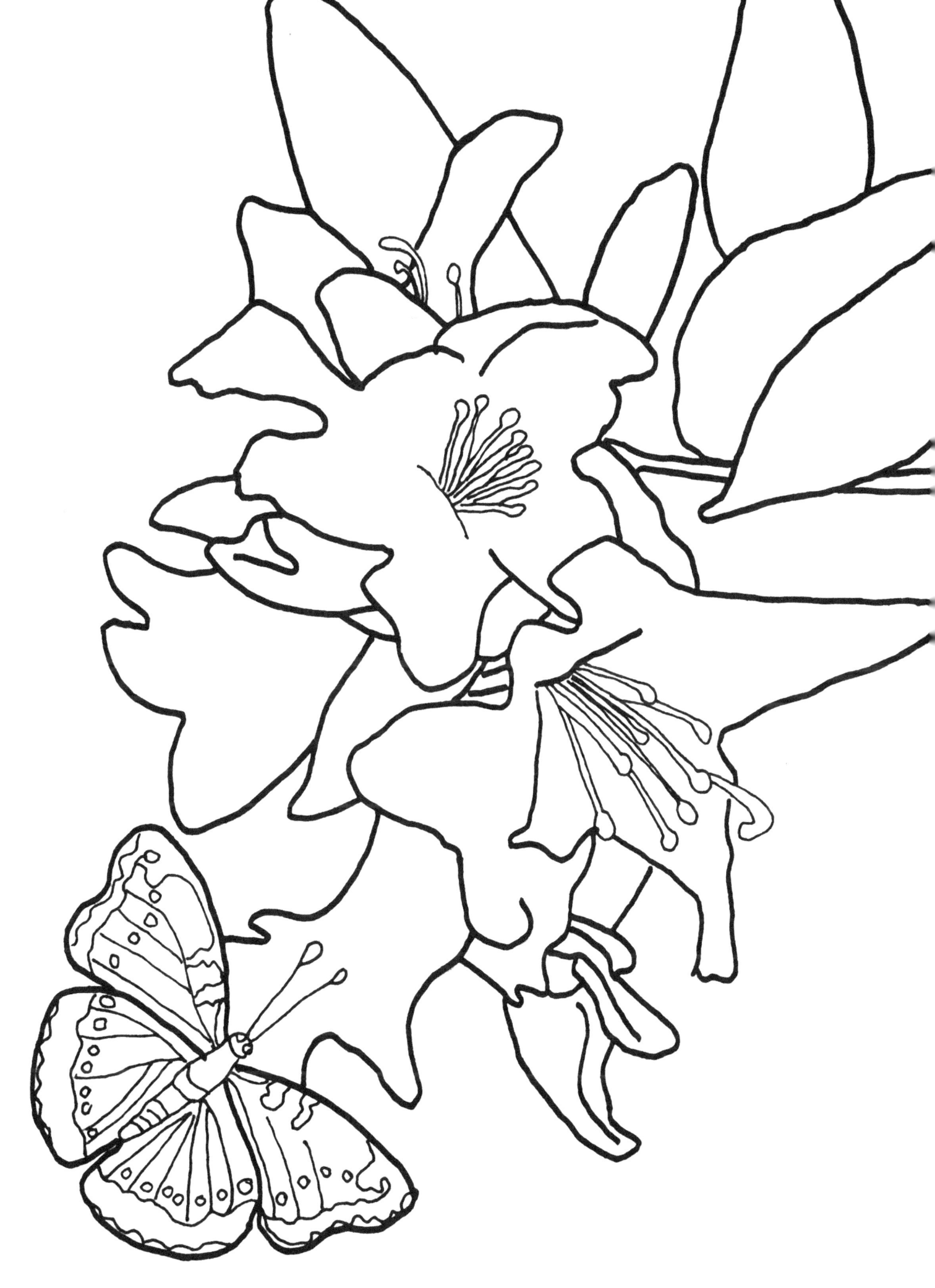

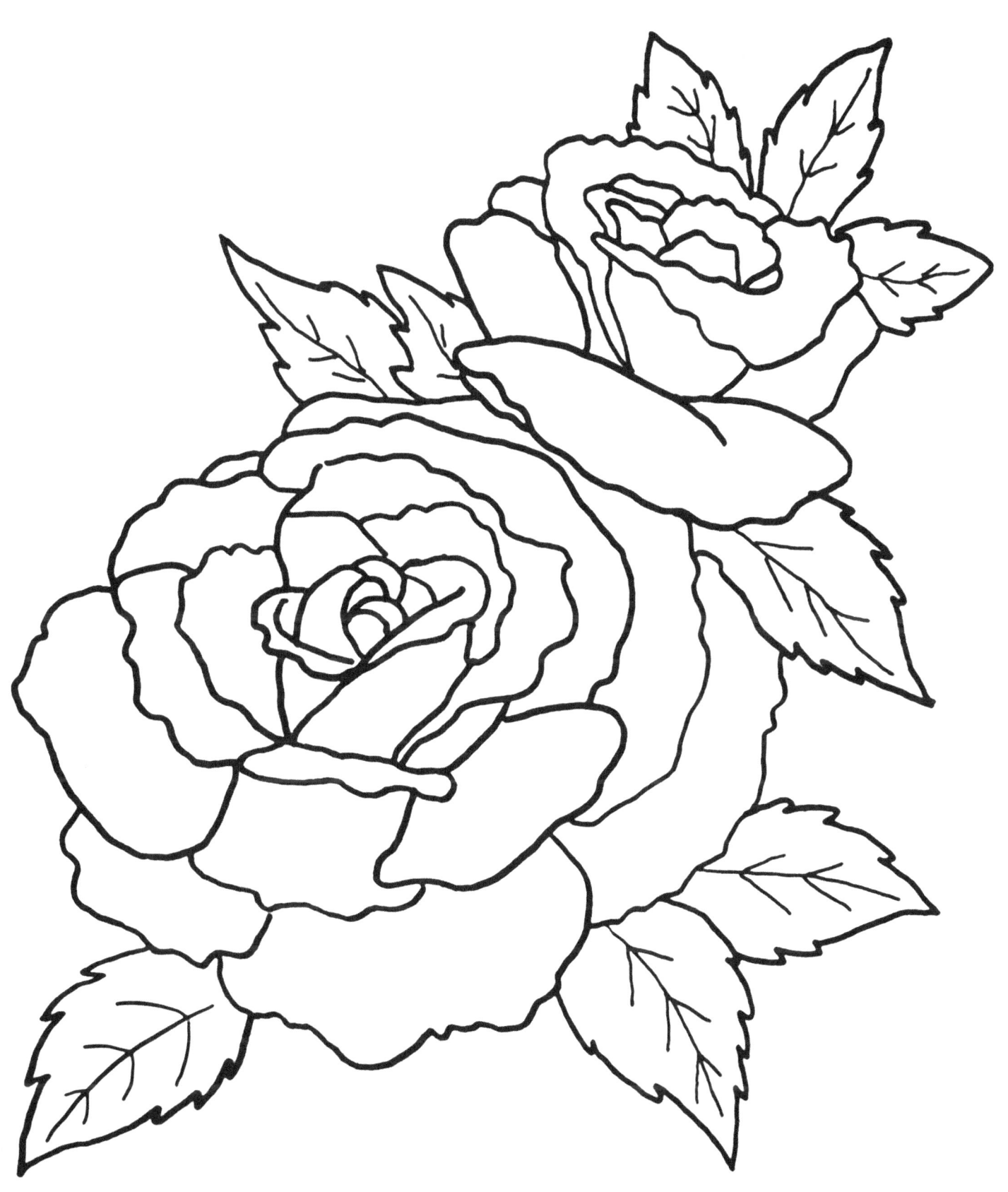

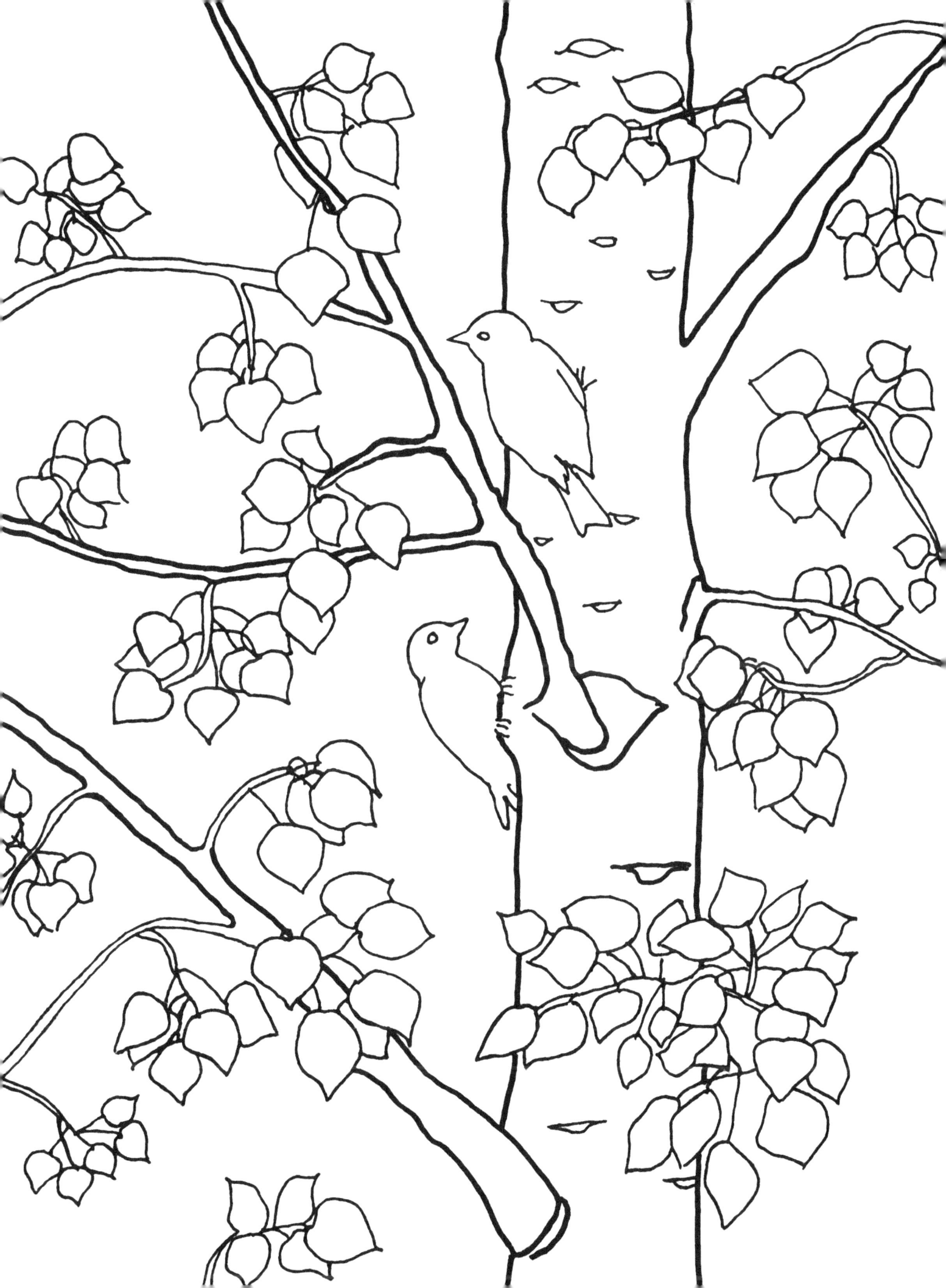

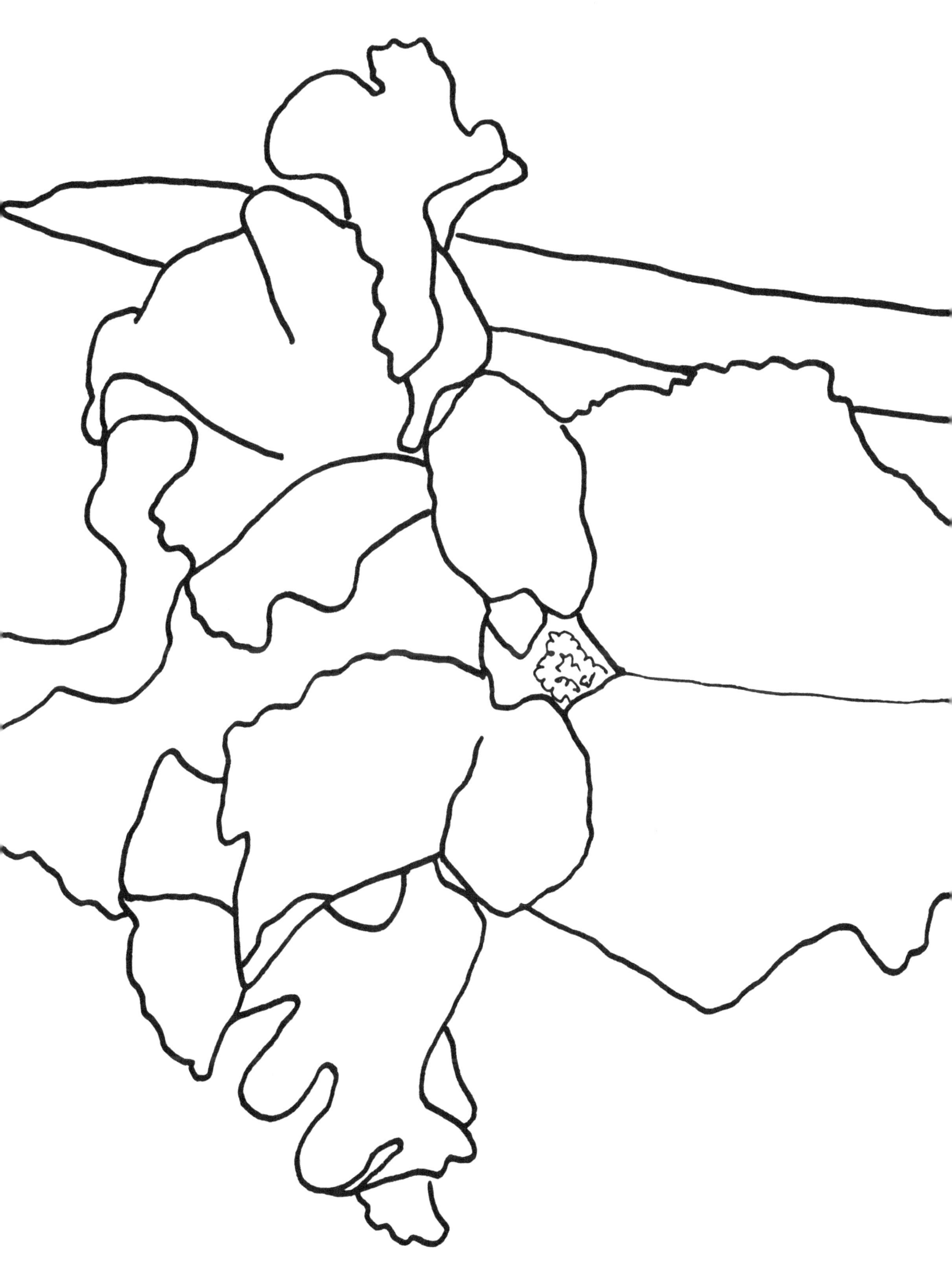

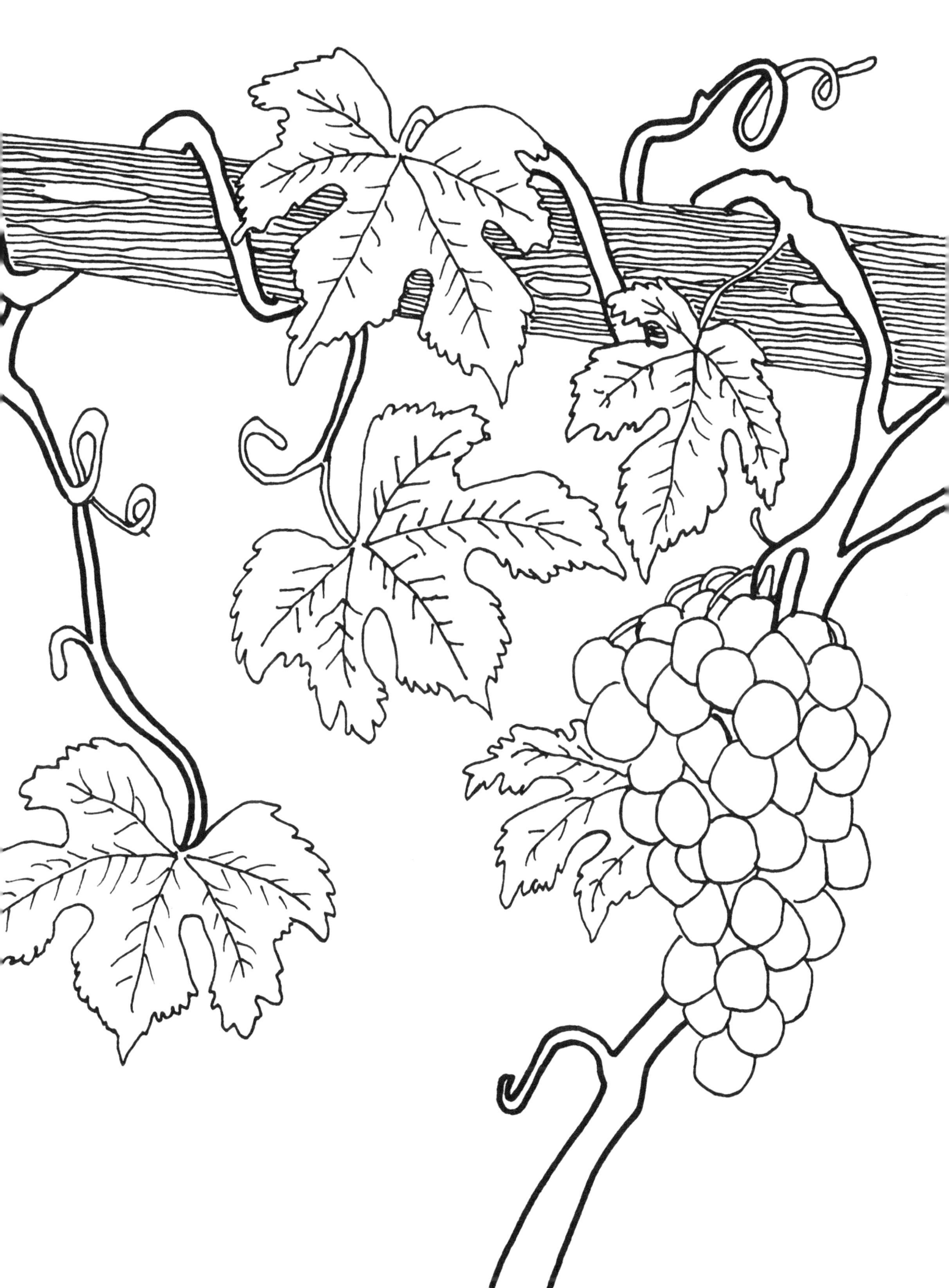

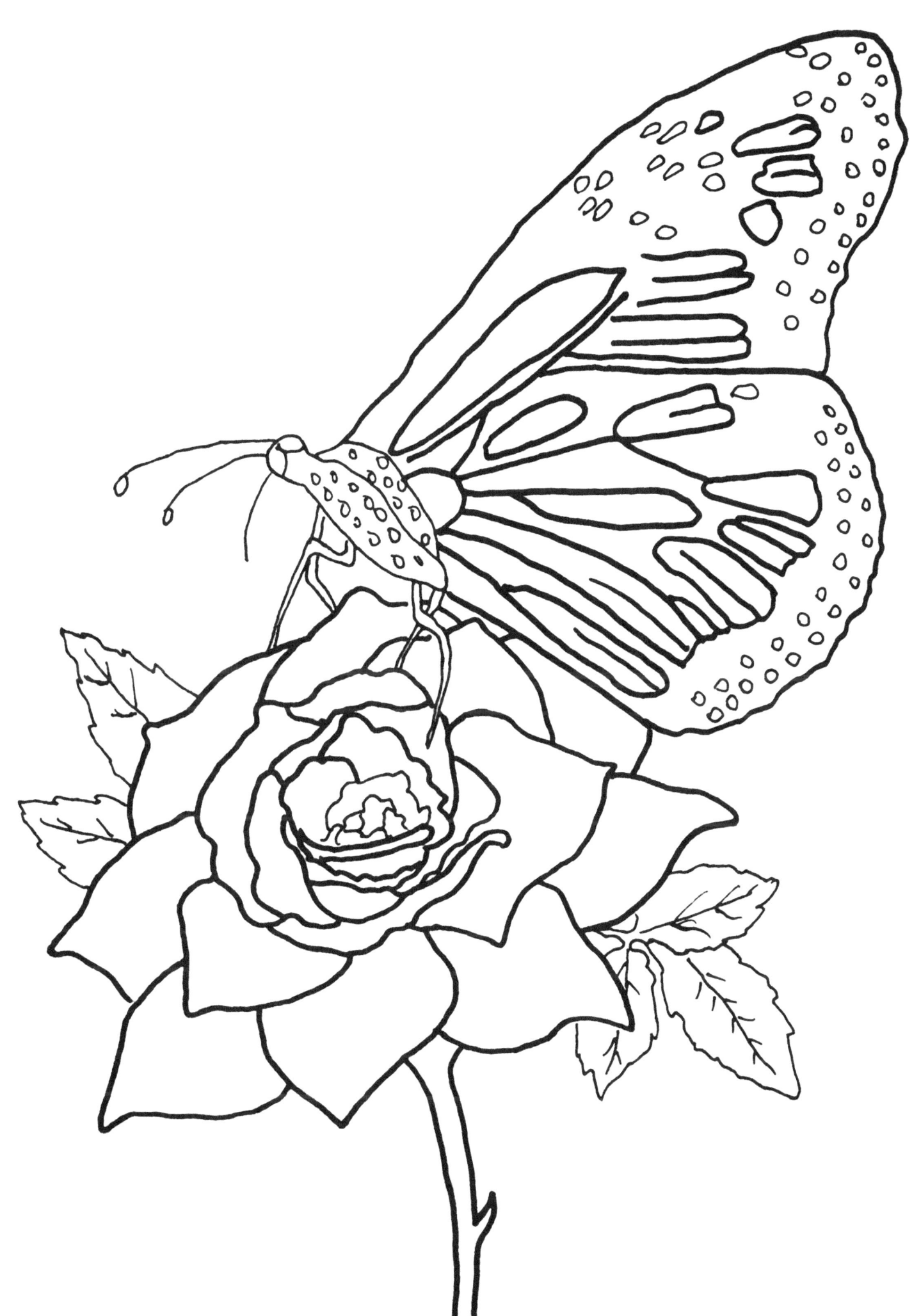

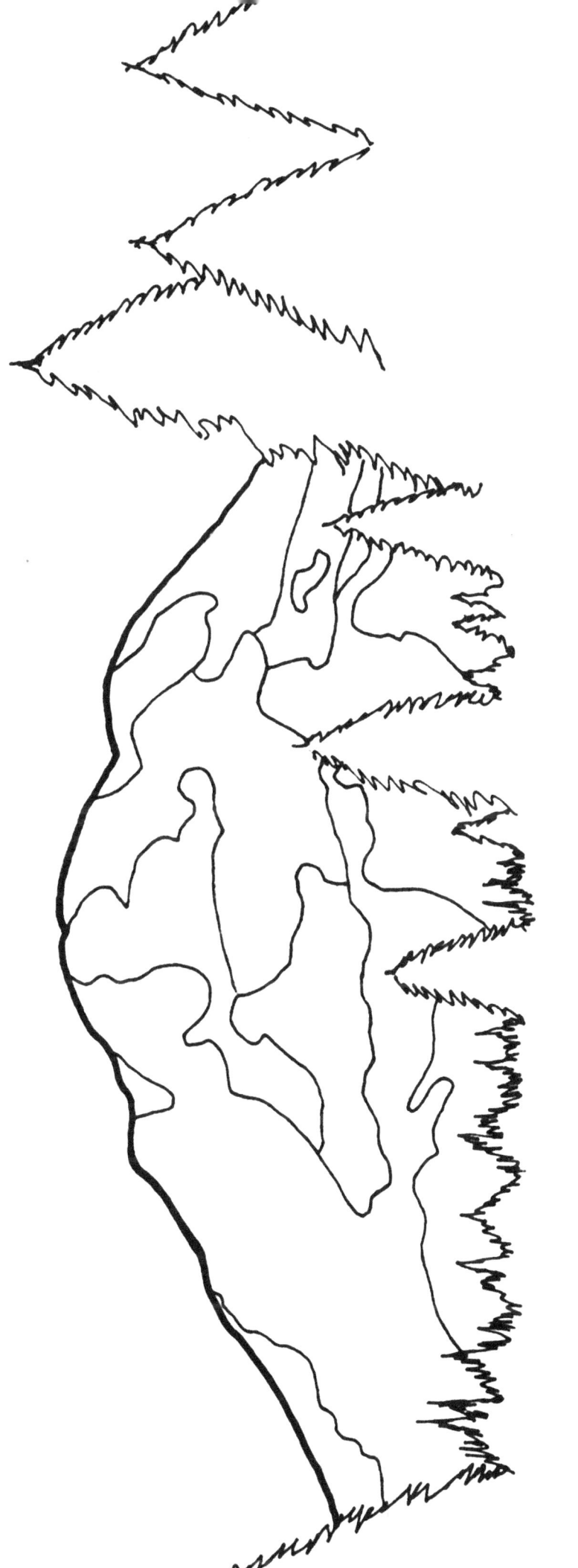

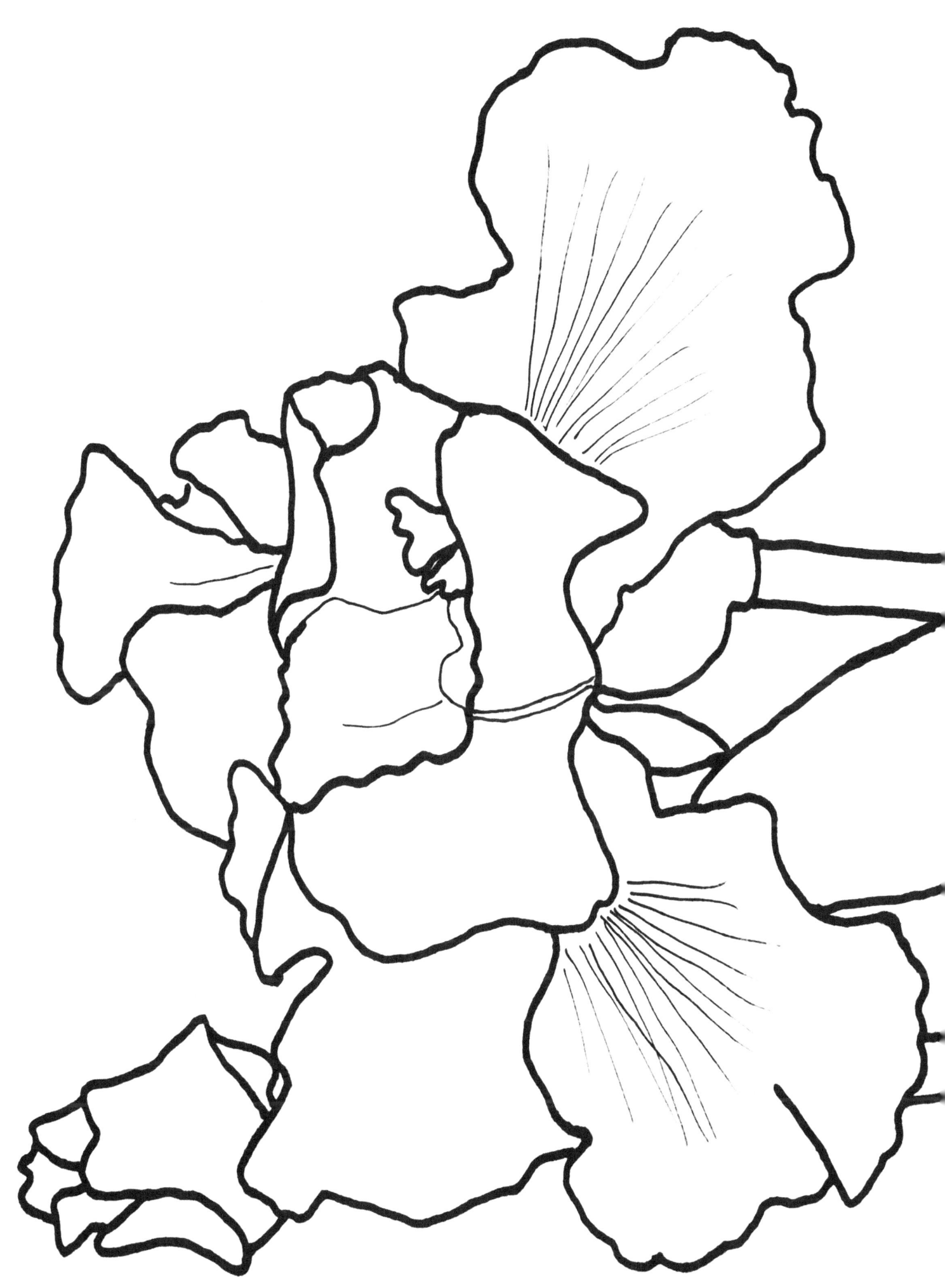

www.ingramcontent.com/pod-product-compliance
Lightning Source LLC
Chambersburg PA
CBHW062341220526
45469CB00008B/2788